FRANKLY SPEAKING...

Insider Advice (Most) Meeting Planners will Never Share with Speakers

Maralynn Adams, CMP

Bonni Scepkowski, SFP

Tracey Smith, CMP, CMM

Shawna Suckow, CMP, SFP

Foreword by Ruby Newell-Legner, CSP

Published by Porcus Volanti (USA)
2211 Marilyn Avenue, St. Paul, Minnesota 55122

ISBN-13: 978-0692788127

ISBN-10: 0692788123

DEDICATION

Maralynn: To this trio of ridiculously hilarious broads - my very own inappropriate Scooby Gang. Who knew making friends after 40 would make me laugh-snort so flippin' often? And to my infinitely patient mom, my awesome boo and my adorable fuzzy pupperino, who keep me sane when planner life makes me crazy...and who do their best to drive me crazy the rest of the time.

Bonni: To this group of unicorns who made me believe that you can make lifelong friends late in life and who make me laugh wine out my nose. I love you with the intensity of 1000 suns. To my sweetie of 16 years who somehow gets me. And who is me. But a guy. And of course, my kids & grandkids who keep me giggling and singing Baby Shark (doo doo doo doo doo doo do).

Tracey: To these three, who keep me sane in an ever-changing industry and world. When the world goes low, they usually go lower and bring me back to reality. And, to my hubby, who has been forced to support the meetings industry for nearly as long as we've been married. No man should understand an attrition clause unless they work in hotel sales. A life sentence.

Shawna: To these three gals, who keep me laughing til something shoots out my nose. I love every one of you with the white-hot intensity of 999 stars. One of mine burned out. Sorry. And to my Shmoopie - here's to 21 more years of bliss. Also to my speaker family at NSA, who inspires me to be better every day - except Fridays. I don't work on Fridays.

CONTENTS

Foreword

by Ruby Newell-Legner, CSP

Inside this treasure-trove of behind-the-scenes conversations, you will learn what is important to the people who hire and work with speakers. To take a sneak peek into the decision-making process is a gift in and of itself. The details you will glean from reading this book will take years off of your learning curve as a professional speaker. These talented meeting planners have been there, done that and have seen it all: the good, the bad, and the ugly! And they are here to share it.

Devour this book with a highlighter and take note of the awareness-developing dialogue that goes on about speakers. Review the top takeaways from each chapter and hold yourself accountable to follow their advice. The payoff will be huge!

This book contains the unspoken strategies of the speaking business. It outlines a step-by-step process speakers need to embrace to get booked, shine on stage, and deliver for meeting planners and their clients.

Woven throughout this book are the answers to these key questions:

- What is the best way to get a meeting planner's attention?
- How do you humanize yourself in a conversation to connect with the planner and be more likable?
- Do you bundle your keynote, workshop, and book signing...or charge separately?
- What are the important elements to include in your demo video/sizzle reel?
- When and how should you share your fees?
- Is a flat travel fee preferred or should you charge for each travel expense?
- When negotiating, what can you do to keep your fee intact?
- Will your interaction with the audiovisual team leave you looking like a professional or a disrespected amateur?
- Do you have to be an author to get booked? If so, how long does your book have to be?
- What thank-you gifts do meeting planners appreciate the most?
- What should you do to recover after making a grievous mistake on stage?
- What behavior gets you called a "Diva" speaker? And

what is a "Divo"?

- What earns you a recommendation from one meeting planner to another, and what makes them "evangelize" for you?

The authors' insights will help you get on the short list and stand out during the selection process. Ultimately their collective wisdom will help you be chosen to speak, prepare for the event, engage with the audience, and be endorsed for additional engagements.

Having to learn all the nuances to succeed as a professional speaker by trial and error will cause you years of struggle and frustration. The truth is, some speakers keep making the same mistakes and fail to grow their business because they do not have the knowledge shared by these gifted meeting planners.

The teachings in this book emulate the authenticity and congruency that you encounter when you meet Shawna Suckow. She is an experienced speaker, an accomplished former meeting planner and a fun person to be around. People just instantly like her.

While volunteering for a non-profit organization with Shawna in Southeast Asia, I fell in love with her style and refreshing transparency. So much so that I selected her to be the only U.S. speaker chosen to present for the International Speaking Day sponsored by the National

Speakers Association when I served as National President. And she did a stellar job.

The respect I have for Shawna easily carries over to her fellow authors. Together they share a powerful combination of experience and wisdom. After 25 of years as a professional speaker, I still took a highlighter to the things I needed to remind myself of. I am sure you will too!

Ruby Newell-Legner, CSP
Fan Experience Expert
www.7starservice.com

President, National Speakers Association 2015-2016
www.NSAspeaker.org

Introduction

"I think this is the beginning of a beautiful friendship."
- Humphrey Bogart in "Casablanca"

This is a series of real conversations between four women with more than 100 years of combined meeting planning experience, not to mention six dogs, six kids, 3 grandkids and more than a few pounds we're trying to lose, but we won't name names. We've all hired our share of speakers, from free all the way up to $200K (plus a private jet for the curious).

Tracey even went to the Bright Side to work for a Speakers bureau for a while, but she came back to planning. Planning is kinda like an old coat that fits really well, makes you look 20 pounds lighter, keeps you really warm, but man, it's a pain in the butt to keep that old coat from shredding into a million pieces. Still, there's no other coat like it. So you keep coming back, like a moth to, well, an old coat.

Maralynn and Bonni still continue to pull their hairs out as planners. They each have owned their own company for about a bazillion years (yet they are somehow still incredibly young, flawless-skinned--did we mention young--women).

After 20 years, Shawna left planning to become a professional speaker back in 2012 (the year the world was supposed to end, according to the Mayan calendar. Update: it didn't).

Ready? Let us begin.

SECTION ONE:

Getting the Gig

"You've got to ask yourself one question: 'Do I feel lucky?'"
- Clint Eastwood in "Dirty Harry"

Chapter One:

Finding Your Niche and Differentiating Yourself

"I have come here to chew bubblegum and kick ass. And, I'm all out of bubblegum."
- Roddy Piper in "They Live"

All: Let's just start this out by explaining that when the four of us get together, hilarity happens. We crack ourselves up, and hope we amuse you a bit with our banter and our random examples. But the information we're sharing is serious and aimed with only the best intentions, to help you understand planners better and to ultimately be more successful and less frustrated with us. So if we drop an example about iguanas or cake (which we likely will), you'll know it's all in fun, but the underlying message is the takeaway. Unless you speak on iguanas, then even better. You do you. #nojudgment

Shawna: So let's dive right in and riff on differentiation. I think it is a critical thing for all speakers, because if planners are searching for you, and you are one of 10,000 people who speak on, say, leadership, then it's going to be really hard for us to discover you. But if you are one of only three people who speak on, say, Leadership in Taco Restaurants, then it's going to be easier to find you when I search. Assuming there's some sort of National Taco Leadership Association, of course.

Bonni: I start my vetting process with Google. If you don't have something specific that makes you stand out and makes me click on your name or your link, then you're going to fall into the forest of the multitudes. If I'm looking for someone who speaks about leadership, how can I tell the difference between you and the zillions of others who do the same? Do you speak about leading teams? Leading different generations? Leading herds of pugs? Every single topic has a million experts. When I go into a bookstore, or on Amazon books, or when I Google a topic, there has to be something specific and different that catches my eye or my ear and differentiates you from everyone else.

Shawna: Good point. How many pages and pages in Google search results do you think there are on, say, Sales Speakers? If you really want to be found, you've got to add a niche or some sort of differentiator so that I can find you if I'm looking for, how about, a Female Sales Speaker, or an African American Sales Speaker who Juggles, or something like that, because we're also focusing more on diversity and uniqueness onstage. What are your differentiators? What makes you unique? How can I find YOU? Why should I choose you?

Tracey: I just googled "Sales Speakers" and 348,000,000 entries popped up. If you don't show up on that first page, see ya!

Bonni: Google your own topic before you decide how you will describe it, because there may be 50 people already who talk about Spaying and Neutering Pugs for Fun and Profit. There may already be someone who has found that specialization, and even if you still want that to be your niche, work on the language that shows what you can do differently. Maybe YOUR pugs wear hats. Maybe you're left-handed. Maybe they are.

Shawna: And I know speakers everywhere are thinking, "If I niche my myself too severely, I'm going to restrict myself." No, I think the opposite is true; I think you increase your findability if you are truly, truly unique. You'll still be found for your overarching topic, but you'll also be found now as THE expert who knows about X, Y, or Z.

Bonni: Exactly. You're not removing yourself from the grander picture, for instance. Keep in mind that when you're making those changes, you're becoming more accessible; different than everyone else. You're not removing yourself from the big pool. You're adding other pools of places where you can be found.

Shawna: Yes, you're adding other search terms that people will be able to find you by, and find you out of a field of sameness among all others.

Maralynn: I think that positioning yourself with your presentation/seminar title is going to help you a lot too. A lot of speakers have very generic presentation titles. When I see something like that on the agenda, I say, "Oh, great. We're going to learn about leadership *again*." Or, "Oh, great, we're going to learn about self-care yet again." But, what if it was "Self-care with Puppies," or something like that? Now, that's going to catch my eye because I'm banana-pants about dogs.

Shawna: Yes! Unique session titles definitely catch my eye. For the annual SPIN conference, for example, we get about 120 submissions for less than 20 session openings. For planners who handle 20 or more conferences a year, we're talking thousands of topic names to sift through! If your session name is boring or too similar to others, it's not helping you stand out in our eyes.

Maralynn: Also, as Shawna mentioned before, there are a lot of speakers who try to appeal to everyone. You're never going to please them all, so if you can find a niche and people who truly appreciate what you have to offer, then you're going to be more successful in the long run. You won't get lost in the shuffle so easily.

Shawna: I see a lot of speakers who want to be all things to all people, and so when I meet someone and I say, "What do you speak on?" And they say, "Oh, leadership, sales, self-care, Jell-O molds, tree pruning, and crockpot cookery. I want to be your speaker, just tell me what you want." That's just so generic and inauthentic. What's your passion? What's your one thing? What's your one thing that you can bring to my audience? I'd rather pick someone who is really well-known for one thing, rather than some generic speaker who wants to mold themselves in my audience's image.

Bonni: But what if you have two passions? What if you want to speak about Jell-O molds AND you are also an expert in puddings? Find an umbrella that encompasses both. "I'm desserts-oriented as a speaker, with a specialty in Jell-O molds, but an ability to also speak about cake." (I've got to go have something to eat now.)

Tracey: Mmm. Cake. Pudding cake.

Shawna: You make a good point, Bonni, because you can always be hired as the keynote for your main topic, but planners love it when you're already there and you are willing to do a breakout on another topic. You may totally pivot in your breakout, and that's okay, but I want to know what your main thing is. What is your main lane, what's your main differentiator, what's your main passion? And then great if you have a bonus as a cake decorator...I'm hungry now, too.

Maralynn: One thing that my dad would always say that makes sense here is, "I don't want you to be the jack of all trades, master of none." I want you to focus on something that, like Shawna mentioned, is your passion, because it's going to be apparent in your delivery. When someone is passionate about something, it's infectious. And when you're not, that comes out too. Like when I talk about dieting.

Shawna: And you don't want to be that guy, where I say, "Oh, you've got to meet my friend Bob, he's a great speaker." And the other meeting planner says, "About what?" "Oh, anything, really. He's just a good speaker." You've got to give me something to refer you by, such as if I have a friend who plans a conference on writing instruments, for example, I'd say, "Bob's a great speaker on the tiny springs within pens, and he knows everything there is to know about pen springs. Like nobody else I've ever heard." That's the kind of thing that makes you more memorable and more referable too. You have an actual niche.

Maralynn: Yes! The topic that you're passionate about doesn't have to be one tiny little thing like, "I love toothpicks!" What you can do is figure out a way to tie that thing to key topics people are looking for and that planners are looking for someone to speak about. Tie those damn pen springs to leadership, or to motivating your team, or whatever that may be. And there are ways to do it, I've seen it done many times, and it's amazing how someone can pull seemingly unrelated topics together.

Shawna: Yes! My friend Kim Becking is using slingshots as a metaphor for change and resilience in her speaking. It's totally eye-catching to planners because it's different. And my other friend Mimi Brown is incorporating deejaying with her leadership topic. They totally stand out.

Maralynn: Exactly. They have figured out a way to give you an analogy, or a little picture, or an animation, or a something that ties it all back together for you, and that makes it memorable. Because you're going to be thinking of that pen spring guy, but you actually learned something greater from the pen spring guy besides the secret life of pen springs.

Shawna: I know speakers out there are going to be thinking, "Well, how does that look on my website, if I'm a pen spring specialist, but I also know everything there is to know about toothpicks?" And you really do have two strengths that are just as good. The way that I see that looking on your website is, your main page focuses on your main passion, and maybe you have a drop down for programs you do about your secondary passions or whatnot.

I know that can get confusing. But always help us understand your main expertise. I know it's hard to choose just one. Because of my planning experience, I'm a hospitality and meetings expert, but now I'm branding myself with the overarching umbrella of consumer behavior. I have a page on my site that's still dedicated to hospitality sessions, but it's not splashed all over my home page. I don't want to confuse anyone.

Tracey: Shawna, I applaud you for that. Listen up, if I can't tell what your main topic is in the first six seconds on your website, you won't make it to the short list. That website needs to be super-easy to get a clear first impression of who you are and what you do in a super-short time frame. We're talking seconds.

Bonni: And we all know that one of the ways to differentiate when you market yourself is by writing articles on your area of expertise. If you want to write something about your combined passion of pen springs and toothpicks, write an article, and have it bring them back to your website. You'll make it easy for us to find you.

Shawna: For me, as a former meeting planner, I don't proactively seek out speaking engagements to audiences of other meeting planners anymore. But I still love that industry, and I still welcome those opportunities, so I still will write about it, blog about it, or seek out opportunities to be interviewed about it, and it is a sub-page on my website, but the main thrust of my page as a speaker is about consumer behavior. So, there are ways to still market yourself for a secondary expertise, if you do feel like you don't want to let go of your mad Jell-O mold skills.

Maralynn: Impressive.

TOP TAKEAWAYS

1. Differentiation is key if you want to be truly findable. Remember, "Sales Speaker" generated 348,000,000 results on Google.
2. You're never going to please everyone, so find a niche and people who truly appreciate what you have to offer. You won't get lost in the shuffle so easily.
3. Boring presentation titles don't catch the eye of meeting

planners. Find a unique angle.

4. We'd rather pick someone who is really well-known for one thing, rather than some generic speaker who wants to mold themselves in our audience's image.
5. Make sure your website shows your main passion and expertise—obviously and quickly—otherwise you've lost us.

BONUS TIP: "Left-Handed Pugs", Self-Care with Puppies", "The Secret Life of Pen Springs"...these topic titles are gold, people. You're welcome.

Chapter Two:
Setting Your Fee

"Show Me the Money!"
- Tom Cruise in "Jerry Maguire"

Shawna: I am going to reveal an insider secret that most meeting planners would probably dislike me sharing with you, and that is: more often than not, your fee is probably too low. I get this all the time, "How do I raise my fee as a speaker?" And what I say to speakers who ask me that, is you just raise your fee, and the market will tell you if it is justifiable or not, based on your brand and your website and your video. The only people who will know what your past fee was are the people who have hired you before. But everybody else, if a meeting planner is finding you out of the blue on Google, or eSpeakers, he or she is not going to know whether your fee is $500, $5,000, or $20,000, until they look a little further and see if your demo reel justifies it, and then they have the conversation with you. So, you most likely can raise your fee, especially in a strong economy.

Tracey: I have to add that speakers bureaus can help with determining your fee, but you have to have a good demo reel. And, like a trailer from a movie, it better have the really good stuff in it.

When I worked for a bureau, we could tell very quickly if a speaker was worth their posted fee. We also consulted with speakers, and oftentimes, they couldn't believe they could ask for more.

Bonni: Please know, however, that we are working within a budget. A planner who is kind may share that information with you. Sometimes a speaker will say to me, "I'm not really sure what to charge for this particular program." And I can say, "Well, I have $10,000." OR, "Although your fee is $10,000, I only have $8,500." I'm always going to offer that information to you, and you have to decide whether or not it's worth it in any particular case, to take less money. If it's in your backyard, I may offer you less money. If I'm in Philadelphia and you're in Philadelphia, I may offer you less money. If it's not enough money, say no. Be prepared to negotiate. Be prepared to say goodbye to the business if it's not valuable to you. Sometimes we can go back to the client and raise the budget for you. But sometimes, it's not a good fit financially.

Shawna: It's easier for you to negotiate down than up, so I say start higher and put yourself out there as a more valuable speaker as well. But be sure not to price yourself out of their search parameters. Make sure that you have a range that is sure to catch all of the price points that you're willing to speak at. It's just like pricing a house, for instance. You need to cushion it a little, but don't price yourself out of your realistically acceptable ballpark for the industries you target.

Maralynn: I think in a lot of cases, just throwing out your fee in general can be really intimidating because you're worried that you've already priced yourself out of the game, and they're going to just make a judgment and move on to somebody else that's cheaper.

Shawna: That's why I advise speakers to never, never, ever give their fee via email. You have to have a conversation, so you can gauge the planner's reaction, and respond immediately. If you email it, you may never hear back if you missed the mark.

Maralynn: If the gig is really compelling because you think attendees at this event may be future clients, you can position yourself in a specific way that doesn't devalue you. Try saying, "Well, normally my fee is $10,000, but I'm excited about this group. I really want to delve into this with you. I understand that you've have a limited budget, so I'm willing to give you a 25% discount because your group is important to me." Or something to that effect. Or, "Because so-and-so referred you, I'm going to give you the friends and family discount."

Position yourself so you don't lose the respect of the planner by saying, "Well, my fee is $10,000, but we can talk about it." Because that devalues you immediately. There are ways that you can position things to make you sound like you're being strategic, as opposed to taking whatever money they have.

Bonni: And further to that very valuable point from Maralynn, share your fee and then wait and see what the planner's reaction is. Never get off the phone without asking the person you're talking to if they're comfortable with that, or if that falls within the range. So, you might say, "My fee is $10,000." And then you move on and discuss the project, and then before you hang up on that call, ask them, "Are we in the same ballpark with our fee?" That's the point at which you might need to negotiate, or they'll tell you, "Yes, we're in the same ballpark." And now you know you can just move on to step 2. But if you hang up at $10,000, without knowing they only have $7,500, then now you've priced yourself out of the market. Give the planner the opportunity to discuss your fee with you.

Shawna: And just know that most meeting planners won't disclose their budget, and if they do, I would say it is very often not accurate, because they want to negotiate, and make themselves look better in the eyes of their clients and stakeholders. So just know that the first number they give you is often not the real number.

Secondly, I would say, before you discount, see if you can offer more value for that original fee. I know Bonni likes to hire authors, so if I were an author and I were pitching Bonni, I might ask her, "I know it may be uncomfortable for you to disclose your budget, but would you be able to give me a ballpark?" And if she says, "$8,500," and my fee is $10,000, I could say, "Well, what if I were to offer you 100 signed books? Could you then do $10,000?" And some planners have a separate budget they can draw from for giveaways, and you might be able to get your fee that way.

And if you have no choice but to decrease your fee to meet their needs, always ask what they can do in return to make up the difference. Will there be video? Are they hiring a photographer who could take some headshots of you? Will there be an opportunity for them to refer you afterward if you do a good job? Can you use the main stage for great video and photos on your own dime, when they're not using it themselves? (this is a great way for newer speakers to get great main-stage footage, by the way) There are lots of things you can ask for in return. And planners are very willing to give those things if it helps them save money, and if what you're asking for doesn't cost them extra.

Bonni: Often I have a budget for your fee, but I also have a budget to buy your books. And that's a different line item. Your expenses are also a different line item. I'm very forthcoming, so I will say, "In addition, I will buy 250 of your books." That might be something you want to ask. "If I am able to lower my fee, would you also be interested in purchasing a book for each attendee as a giveaway? And I'd be happy to stay the extra time to do a book signing."

Shawna: Let's talk about bundling in travel. Do you prefer when speakers give you a flat fee that includes all their travel, so that they don't have to invoice you after the event? If they say, "My fee is $8,500, and I have a flat travel fee of $1,000." Do you like that, or would you prefer that they itemize, and then you have to cut another check afterward?

Tracey: Flat is sooo much easier! One and done.

Maralynn: I prefer itemization, just because it's transparent. I know it's a second step, but I would like to know what things cost, especially if I'm paying for travel. Whether my speaker is driving in or flying in, I think it's fairer to both sides to do it that way. If you set your fee and for some reason airfares go way up or there's a giant city-wide event, you may spend more on travel than you expected, and you end up getting the raw end of the deal. So for me personally, I prefer the transparency of straight expenses.

Bonni: I agree with Maralynn (again). I prefer to make the travel arrangements and pay for your airline ticket, and maybe use my comped room nights for them, or put it onto the master bill. That's a way I can mitigate the expenses to my client. We'll pay for your Uber or taxi, we'll welcome you to eat with us and make sure you're fed. I do find it to be a bit much when people say, "Well, I ate lunch at the airport at 3pm and I want to expense that back." I'll never forget the expense report that included mints purchased at the airport. I try to be really generous with your meal expenses. If you come in late and want to order room service, that's realistic and fair, but it will leave a bad taste in your client's mouth (no pun intended) if you charge back for every mint.

I don't like to think that you're making money off of your travel allowance. However, if you want to manage and include your travel, you're better off raising your fee a little bit. So if your fee is $5,000, make it $6,000, inclusive of travel. Then you can do what you want with that extra money.

It comes out the same in the end, but it feels more transparent and more comfortable.

Shawna: I know that some planners who have booked me as a speaker like the known entity of a flat travel fee, because it will never go higher than that, and so I take on the risk of my travel expenses exceeding that number. I am terrible about invoicing for my expenses afterward, so if I can get a planner to agree on whatever that travel number is, I prefer it.

The majority of planners I've worked with have accepted my flat fee, and being able to budget in advance for exactly what it's going to cost with no surprises.

Maralynn: I get it.

Bonni: I like it when the speakers give me a flat fee across the board for the speaking portion, though. It does tend to be negotiable if the program changes. If we start from the beginning with keynote with a workshop and a book signing, I want one number for that. However, if you quote a rate for a keynote, and I add a workshop, and another day or another session, then obviously we need to renegotiate. We realize that your time is valuable, and I never want you to undervalue yourself.

Maralynn: I think that you could also put limits on it. You could say, "This is for a keynote, and up to two half-hour sessions. I have a la carte pricing for anything beyond that." Or something worded a bit more eloquently.

Bonni: On the other hand, don't punch a time clock. I had a speaker once try to charge me extra for to stay for lunch and network with the group, when it was actually an invitation for them to join us for lunch. I wasn't asking them to come and hang out as a star attraction, I was actually just inviting them to join us for lunch, because that's what nice people do, and they countered with a fee. I had to clarify, and that wasn't comfortable for anyone.

Shawna: Oh, my God. We need to talk about that in our chapter on diva speakers. I can't believe that they wanted to charge you for the privilege of having them join you for lunch, when in fact, they should be wanting that extra networking time and visibility, because it can lead to additional bookings and build more rapport with the audience. That is just insane. I can't believe that happened.

Maralynn: Yeah, I find this with most of the supplier partners that I work with. When we're in initial conversations and we're talking about fees and other related items, the more you can position yourself as a part of the team or as a partner, the more attractive you will be. "We're all in this together and I want to make this a successful program for you, for me, and for everyone." sounds WAY better than, "I'm this entity on high that has given you the privilege of letting your people hear me speak."

The best speakers I've ever seen or experienced can tie everything together. They remember people's names, they attend meals, they're popping up at...whatever. And granted, not every speaker can do that. Some of them have to fly in and fly out same day. But the more you can create a partnership, the more things will bode well for you. Because when we're having those initial conversations and I'm dealing with a speaker who's unyielding and charging for every little thing, and I've also got a speaker who's like, "It's all about teamwork, it's all about you and me, and it's all about making this the best program possible", that's what I'm going to gravitate toward. Because the person who's being difficult or nitpicky is just demonstrating how the rest of my experience with them is going to go.

Shawna: And frankly, which of those two speakers are you more likely to refer to your meeting planner friends? If somebody's being a complete nitpicky jerk, I don't want them to get future business by working with my friends, and I don't want my friends to have to deal with that kind of stress at their events.

Bonni: I've had speakers who come to the evening cocktail reception the night before their keynote, and then go back to their room and redo their slides, because they've gotten to know the people and the personality of the group. I love those speakers. Maybe after meeting the group they want to be more casual, or maybe they want to be a bit more corporate. Maybe they've learned there's a common thread or a common question that runs through the group. Any pre-speaking time that you get to spend with the audience should be a valuable gift to you. Those are the speakers that I respect the most, and the ones who are the most successful.

Tracey: One last comment. The contractual agreement should address the amount of time the speaker will be available onsite. What it says to me, as a planner and former bureau person, is that you, the speaker, belong to the event for that time. I shouldn't find you lounging at the pool or working in your room if my program is going on. Outside of those hours is your own time, but see if the planner can give you more exposure while you're there.

TOP TAKEAWAYS

1. If you're wondering if it's time to raise your fee, it probably is! Just make sure you have the branding and quality video to back it up.
2. If you must discount your fee to get a gig, always ask the planner what they may be able to offer you in return.
3. The more you can position yourself as a partner, the more attractive you will be. "We're all in this together and I want to make this a successful program for you, for me, and for everyone." sounds WAY better than, "I'm this entity on high who has given you the privilege of letting your people hear me speak."
4. If a speaker is a complete nitpicky jerk, we don't want them to get future business by working with our planner friends, so we'll never refer them.

BONUS TIP: Don't expense mints or charge us when we ask you to join us for lunch. Don't be the pooper at the party.

Chapter Three: Speakers Bureaus

"I'm gonna make him an offer he can't refuse."
- Marlon Brando in "The Godfather"

Shawna: So, ladies, what do you think about working with bureaus? Do you utilize them?

Bonni: I work with speakers bureaus quite a bit. Sometimes it's easier to speak directly with the speaker. I prefer to have a back-and-forth conversation and get to know the person and get a feel for their conversation style. A lot of planners are too busy and need someone to vet speakers for them. Often the kind of content I'm searching for is not that common, and it makes it difficult for a speakers bureau to come to me with someone who fits these weird little niches that I'm looking for. I've already done the research. I'm already looking, I've found you and I want to talk to you to see if we've got a good fit. Sometimes a speakers bureau can be a block between me having a conversation with the speaker, but 9 times out of 10 they are a great resource.

Shawna: You are not seeking out a speakers bureau to help you in those instances. Rather, you have no choice because the speaker is exclusive to a particular bureau? I'm guessing that's because of the fee range you're working in, for some of your speakers. The higher the fee range, the more likely they are to have, quote-unquote, "representation."

Bonni: Yeah, that's very often the case. Having said that, there are speakers bureaus I work with that I will call when I'm not getting anywhere on my own, and I really need a professional hand. "I need somebody who speaks about this." And they might know those speakers well enough to be able to say, "Oh, well, Shawna Suckow speaks about blah, but she can modify that...she speaks about staples, but maybe she can address 'Staples as the

21st-Century Office Staple' or "She can speak about Pez dispensers and their role in millennial employee satisfaction." So, there's a great value to a great speakers bureau. I guess my point is I work both ways. I love and respect my bureaus, but really like to spend time getting to know that speaker.

Shawna: As a planner, I loved when I worked with a good speakers bureau to help me source really interesting speakers, but like you, if I find a good speaker or if I've heard a good speaker, I will just go direct if the option exists. But I know a lot of planners do enjoy working with bureaus because it cuts down on their workload.

Bonni: I have to have the time to be able to do that kind of research. Otherwise the speakers bureau is indispensable. And most planners don't have the time. If they're busy and they're successful, they don't have the kind of time to put into the research.

Shawna: I like how you used the word "indispensable" in the same section as Pez dispensers. So, good job there.

Bonni: I thank you!

Maralynn: Not having hired as many speakers as say, Bonni has, a speakers bureau is probably going to be one of the first places I look, along with reaching out to colleagues for recommendations.

For example, with SPIN [Senior Planners Industry Network], there are a lot of planners who've experienced many different speakers and can recommend people directly. I'd say that being a part of a speakers bureau should be one of the tools in your toolbox. Especially when you're establishing yourself and trying to get the word out there, it'll be pretty important for them to evangelize for you.

But, I agree with Bonni that my first inclination, having booked actors before for filming, is that I would much rather go direct than deal with their agent, for obvious reasons. For right or wrong, that's the direction I'll start in because I'm trying to get the best product and the best price for my client. BUT, I'm not going to cheat a speakers bureau. If they found me a great speaker, then I'm going to stay loyal to them.

Bonni: Yes. Yes. Yes. I would never, ever try to cut someone out if they've done the work. Never, ever try to go around your bureau if they have brought you business. Have some respect for their part in your success. But make sure your speakers bureaus understand where your lines are, and where you're flexible, where you are open to modification, because I've had bureaus turn me down on behalf of speakers because I'm a couple thousand dollars off on budget, or because I won't do first class airfare ever, ever, in the continental US, and perhaps you feel open to those changes.

Bonni: Those are times when your bureau is trying to protect you, but may close a door for you that might have been appealing to you. Let them know where you're flexible. Because they'll fight for you.

Shawna: But also, make sure your bureau or whoever is recommending you is on the same page ethically, as well. I recently presented a flat travel fee to a new-to-me bureau, and the bureau put in the agreement with the client that I wanted a certain amount of dollars every day in addition, for meals, and all sorts of other things I never would ask for, because my all-inclusive travel fee is just that: all inclusive. The client contacted me about it and thought I was maybe trying to be a little bit shady, when in fact, that did not represent me at all. So, just be careful you're all on the same page, and they're representing you in the way you want to be represented.

Bonni: Yeah. On that same note, I would expect the same transparency from your speakers bureau as we expect from you. Make sure you understand the contract they've created on your behalf. Ask to see, at least the boilerplate contract they're using on your behalf, and make sure it represents your values and what you need and what you want. And if there's something there you're not comfortable with, they've got to take it out. They are representing you. Keep an eye out for those green M&M riders.

Tracey: Having worked as a bureau rep, I can tell you they can be indispensable when it comes to the problems that arise. If a speaker becomes ill or has a serious travel delay, the bureau will help find another speaker on the spot. The bureau will know who a suitable replacement would be, and oftentimes the replacement can be better.

There was one case where a speaker I had booked became terminally ill. Another speaker who was a friend of this guy offered to take on his bookings at no extra charge. The sub-speaker's fee was double normally, so the client got a major bang for their buck. I have also had the booking where the speaker got nasty with the planner and I had to step in to mediate the situation. So bureaus do earn their keep! And, they typically do not add fees onto the speaker's fee. The commission comes out of the speaker fee. I liken the speakers bureau to an automobile dealership. It's highly unusual a buyer would go directly to the manufacturer, and also highly unusual the buyer would get service from the manufacturer. It's good to have that buffer and let them do a lot of the work for you.

Shawna: I know one of the major questions I had as a newer speaker was how to get noticed by bureaus. My advice would be to network with the reps at industry functions, and invite them to come and see you speak if you're in their town for a gig. Also be on the lookout for bureaus who do periodic showcases – those generally require a fee from newer speakers to be showcased to an audience of the bureau's clients, along with several other speakers at one event. Lastly, you've got to really work on your niche to be findable to bureaus, just like with planners. Don't lump yourself in generically with other speakers who are better known; differentiate to get noticed.

TOP TAKEAWAYS

1. Make sure your speakers bureaus understand where your lines are, and where you're flexible, where you are open to modification.
2. Those are times when your bureau is trying to protect you, but may close a door for you that might have been appealing to you.
3. Don't rely solely on bureaus for work. Some planners prefer to contact you directly.
4. The more you niche yourself, the more you'll catch the eye of a bureau who's trying to fill a specific need for a planner.

BONUS TIP: "Staples as the 21st-Century Office Staple," "Pez Dispensers and Millennial Employee Satisfaction"...scoop these session ideas up, y'all! You can thank Bonni for these quality nuggets.

Chapter Four:

Being Findable in the Right Way

"Wait a minute, wait a minute. You ain't heard nothin' yet!"
- Al Jolson in "The Jazz Singer"

Shawna: Gals, how important is it for a speaker to be an author?

Tracey: When I was at the speakers bureau, it was actually very important for speakers to have a book because it made them more serious about being a speaker as opposed to someone who is just in it for the fun of it. That was one thing I always used when I sold speakers, or promoted speakers to planners...that they had a book. Either that, or they have the CSP [Certified Speaking Professional designation, bestowed by the National Speakers Association],we that's another thing because it means they have booked the hours in that profession. If they had their CSP, I always used that as a selling tool.

"This person has a CSP so therefore they're more professional and they know what they're doing." That was part of it.

Shawna: I know when I was a newer speaker, writing my first book made all the difference. It just gave me huge credibility that I don't think I had before, so I totally agree with you, Tracey.

Bonni: Same. Generally, I find a book before I find the speaker. I'm googling a subject, I'm looking for specific content, I'm looking for that expert or the person who's got some knowledge, and generally, I will find that through a book or an article someone has written. It's very rare that I'll go straight to a speakers bureau and book that way. I do go to bureaus, if that's what I need to do, but generally I'm looking at the book, I'm looking at the subject matter and, just as a counterpoint, for me, I don't necessarily look for a CSP. My clients don't know what that means. My speakers are generally content-based. They've written some book, they're out there promoting that book and they may have followed a different path.

Maralynn: I think that goes back to being findable in the right way. I suspect a lot of people use Amazon. One of the things that I've used in the past with Amazon is their book previews. Many times, they will give you previews of the first few pages of each chapter, or at least a few pages of the book to give you a feel for it.

Also, I think having your own website is extremely important. They can't all be as amazing as Shawna's, but you've got to start somewhere. I think making yourself findable--here's how you reach me, here's all my contact information, etc. is crucial. And, "Here's where I'm going to be speaking" is good. Typically, you're probably booking private gigs, but there may be an opportunity where someone can come to get a feel for what you're doing and how you present yourself and whether you use magic or toys.

Bonni: Along that same note, you have to have good video. Work on that. I just had a fascinating speaker turned down by my client because he was just far too academic and dry on his Ted Talk. He really just needed some training. I told him because it seemed like the right thing to do, and I hope he follows through because his content was perfect.

Tracey: I hear you, Bonni. The video is absolutely the primary thing. That gives us an insight into that person's personality. However, one thing I find about being likable is you can now go to the speakers bureau website and type in leadership, and it comes up with 150 speakers. I need to find someone who is in leadership for women, or leadership for college graduates, or something like that where it's a little bit more defined. The more a speaker can define their topic and not just some blanket category, the better.

Bonni: I am often looking up a very specific topic. I am not looking for a leadership speaker, or a sales speaker, or a motivational speaker. I just found a speaker I was seeking for by Googling "lifecycle of a business." I was looking for someone who has gone from entrepreneurship to success and I didn't want the motivation part. I didn't want a story that said 'and you can do this too!' I wanted them to talk about how business changes, about the process. I wanted takeaways for our guests to apply. I wanted to hear about their failures and successes during the process, and I used all of that in my search. It was a tough find, but I found my speaker.

Maralynn: YouTube is a huge help for searching for topics. Make the titles of your videos very specific. There are a lot of opportunities out there. You might be speaking about the life cycle of slugs and snails or something similar that people are interested in. YouTube can give you a lot of different options as long as you select tag words. Use all that you've got. Make sure the title is something interesting and don't be afraid to throw in some interpretive dance.

Bonni: Definitely throw in some interpretive dance.

Shawna: Who says slugs are not interesting? I find slugs doing interpretive dance to be fantastically entertaining...but back to YouTube. Yes, YouTube is the second most used search engine after Google, and Google indexes YouTube in its results. You have to have your own YouTube channel today and populate it with videos of you, plus video testimonials from people who've seen you speak and loved you. Video is the direction we are moving as a society. But you still need a book. Even if you only have a simple, short book, it is still better than no book.

I have several speaker friends who are doing a short tip book for their first book. Like "52 Tips on Wellness", for example. The credibility is priceless, plus you have something to give away or sell at the back of the room.

Tracey: In addition to that, I'm not sure what the correct term is. Google ads or ads on Facebook. If you type in something, suddenly all that crap pops up. Like shoes, all of a sudden all these ads for shoes pop up. I was looking for a bathing suit and I got like nine million. I'm still getting ads for bathing suits. Things like that where if you can tie in something with your video to it, that would be very key, I would think.

Shawna: That fun tactic is called "re-targeting." It's a little creepy, I think, that those unicorn slippers I searched for are turning up everywhere I look online now...

Maralynn: I like what Shawna referenced with the testimonials, too. I think it can be extremely impactful for people to give their perspective on what they liked, in a video.

Tracey: You have to be careful with testimonials. I had one speaker who did not have a video or anything I could use to determine if he was any good. So, I called him and asked for a video. He didn't have one, and said his testimonials speak for themselves. Really? They were written on his website. Do you really think I believe that? The only written testimonial I will believe is from someone I know. Period.

Maralynn: Also audio is important. I think there's an advantage to offering an audio version of your book or your blog so we can hear how you engage. What is your voice like? Do you deliver everything monotone? Do you sing all of it? What is your demeanor? Potential clients can play your audiobook in their car during traffic and just listen to your mellifluous speaker voice. An audio version can be an advantage because folks can listen to it in their spare time or just catch a quick five minutes.

Bonni: Agreed on every point. I'm just going to agree with everything Maralynn says from here until the day I die. I'm just going to go ahead and get a tattoo that says "samesies" that I can show every time Maralynn says something.

The tone of your voice, those mellifluous tones that Maralynn spoke of are so important. Better than someone who has been trained to stand in front of a room and use all of those hand motions and arm things you learn in speaker training (right now just for those of you who aren't watching me in my living room, visualize my arms outstretched and then my hands are clasped together...now I'm doing the international symbol for synergy). The tone of your voice and the conversational way of speaking are the most important skills when it comes to driving audience attention.

Shawna: Let's shift to blogs and social media as an umbrella for findability. How important is it for a speaker to have a blog or have you found speakers because of their blogs?

Bonni: I have. All the livelong day I find speakers through blogs.

Shawna: 'Livelong day?' Do you now work on the railroad, old timer?

Bonni: I do. Again, I'm looking for a subject. I'm not looking for a general umbrella of stuff you talk about. If I'm looking for an expert on the role of Bird Feeders in Urban Planning and you have a blog that touches on it, you've won the game. I've found best-selling authors through a blog they wrote three years before their book came out that has nothing to do with their book title. It tells me not only can they speak and write, but they can address that specific topic. Yeah, definitely blog.

I'm more inclined to take you seriously if you are writing articles on LinkedIn than Facebook, by the way. I still see Facebook as where you hang out with your friends and LinkedIn is where you run your business.

Maralynn: I think the blog posts help, because they are a marketing tool. You can post those on LinkedIn occasionally or you can use them as a response to a group you belong to that's discussing that exact issue. "I wrote a post about this last year, here's a link to it, this may help." There are a lot of ways to work your way into people's brains, like a worm.

Tracey: One other thing that I think really helps is if you are in the news. [Laughter from the group] A lot of speakers, no seriously though, our bureau got requests for a lot of speakers because they had made the news somehow. A good example might be the kids who were trapped in Thailand in the cave. When they finally got them out, the young man who was the leader could be really hot as a speaker because he had a story to tell. That was another thing. Being in the news, if you can, it's helpful.

Bonni: That will also bring all these spelunking experts to the forefront.

Shawna: Bonni gets bonus points for the word Spelunking. Okay, let's talk a little bit more about social media. How important are the various social media tools? Now, Bonni, you mentioned LinkedIn, and you mentioned Facebook is not as business-y, how do you feel about Twitter and Instagram?

Bonni: LinkedIn is my go-to for business. That doesn't mean if you post something really interesting and really brilliant on Facebook that I'm not going to see it and take it seriously. It elevates you if you're on LinkedIn, but that doesn't mean to not use Facebook.

Twitter I find great. If someone's tweeting out interesting little topics over and over again, they've caught my eye. Instagram, I'm too old to use. (hangs head in shame)

Maralynn: I'm too old too, but I actually jumped on Instagram within the last year to market a film. I figured that I should since it's there for the using. I think there's different audiences for each one. LinkedIn is obviously legit business, if you are business-oriented.

It doesn't hurt to throw things up on Facebook, but if you are representing yourself by using a business page, you may not get the exposure that you're looking for.

The chances that people will see posts from your business page are slim and they keep getting slimmer. Facebook has created so many blocks because they want to charge you to get in front of people. Businesses are just frustrated that they are not getting to their audiences.

I don't utilize Twitter and I really should. I have so many different social media time-sucks in my life and I can only juggle so many at a time.

With Instagram, I'd say the approach could be a bit more aspirational. You're going to need to use images and maybe inspirational text, just don't become annoying with the generic inspirational sayings. Small video clips are good, as long as they are 59 seconds or less. Bits and pieces like that can make you compelling. Anything short and sweet is recommended because people flip by Instagram posts really quickly. One drawback is that you can't list a URL on an Instagram post. You have to put the URL in a link in your bio on your main profile page. Hopefully that'll change someday, but for now, it's a pain in the butt. I find it strange that

Facebook also owns Instagram because the difference between them and the success of getting your message out on each one is considerable.

Shawna: It really all depends on the types of audiences you're targeting as a speaker, and where they hang out on social media. I tend to think of LinkedIn and YouTube as the two go-to sites for me as a speaker. LinkedIn and YouTube, people can find me by searching for a particular topic. As long as the speaker is using appropriate hashtags, like Maralynn was saying. Hashtag it, describe it well. I have a social media guru I work with and she just gave me a tip that I never thought of. On my YouTube channel, I have a million testimonials and videos, but I never once in the description put, "Hire Shawna to speak on these topics and here's her website". Duh.

Bonni: Duh.

Maralynn: Duh, of course. But, one thing Instagram does well is that it gives you the option to follow a hashtag. That hashtag will come up in your feed no matter what. For example, I may possibly be inclined to follow #chocolatecake and if I've chosen to follow it, any posts using #chocolatecake will pop in my feed. You can even look up how many posts have been created using that hashtag and the higher the number, the better.

You can use #speaker, which will have a ton of posts. Or, you can use #slugspeaker, which will not have a ton of posts, but remember what we said about being findable for your specific niche. There may very well be people following that specific hashtag and if you just hashtag all of your posts with it, you could build fans.

Bonni: The hashtag #slugspeaker comes up on my daily feed [laughs]. I think something like Instagram works better if you are a more of a motivational speaker. I see that more. Not to imply she's purely motivational, but Meridith Elliott Powell does beautifully with her posts. It's generally a great quote and a picture of her gorgeous face. She always has something compelling to say that drives me back to her website for more inspiration. Otherwise, I'm not looking at Instagram unless I am looking at motivational, which it not usually my area.

Tracey: I'm not a big Instagram user either, but I do follow certain people because we're related or whatever. I do think that, Shawna you are really good about posting selfies with your audiences. You know, the one you just spoke to. I always find those interesting and I don't know why, but to me it's like you are connected to those people now, either because you just spoke to them or because you transformed them somehow.

I like that. It's connects me a little bit as well.

Shawna: That's funny, my new website designer said, "Quit sending me pictures of you on stage taking a selfie with some other random group. I have enough." I'm like, "I like it! It's my thing!"

Bonni: I have to say, better than a testimonial, is that image of people smiling with you after you are done speaking, and they obviously love you. There's always going to be a question when you have a testimonial, as to how legit it is, but you can't question the big goofy love faces on the audience after you've done your slug speech.

Tracey: It's specifically the ones where Shawna is in another country. It's a different culture and they are all smiling and are reacting or dancing with you or whatever. That, to me, says a lot. You have connected with that group.

Maralynn: I think both Facebook and Instagram are more temporary in nature than what Shawna was talking about with LinkedIn and YouTube. One advantage is that if you have time, both Facebook and Instagram have incorporated "stories." Instagram stories last for 24 hours. They're up and then they're gone. They are trying to be Snapchat in some sense. Now, because Facebook owns both, your Instagram story can now be simultaneously posted to Facebook. This gives you two different areas to market in and it's just another way to quickly engage.

Shawna could also take a video with the crowd. You could say, "Hey everybody, for two seconds we're going to say hello to everyone in my Instagram story, blah, blah, blah." You record it right there and boom it's up. Anyone watching the stories option will actually see you in Tokyo, or Dubai, or wherever you happen to be speaking and they can see everyone cheering for you. The audio on that is also compelling.

Bonni: Don't forget your personal life is not necessarily off-limits. If you are doing volunteer work, if you're doing something cool and interesting and unique, it just shows you as a more well-rounded person. I mean, personally, I love Maralynn mainly because she gives me access to Martini, her dog. Sometimes, what you are doing is interesting and compels me to want to engage with you. Shawna, your travels to South America this past year were fascinating to watch, and not only did I learn, I wanted to hang out with you.

Shawna: That's a perfect transition for our next chapter on being likable.

TOP TAKEAWAYS

1. Having a book is essential for credibility as a speaker today.
2. A well-defined niche and great video make you findable and likeable.
3. A YouTube channel is critical today to increase your findability.
4. Video testimonials are more trusted than written testimonials.
5. Choose the social media where your target demographic spends the most time. Use hashtags for findability.
6. Don't be afraid to share personal stuff to be more memorable and establish a true connection.

BONUS TIP: Hastags to consider include #chocolatecake (always a winner), #slugspeaker (this could be HUGE), #livelongday (yeehaw!), #interpretivedance (people LOVE that), #mellifluousspeakervoice (practice practice practice!)

Chapter Five: Being Likeable

"I like your style, kid, I really do."
- Richard Dreyfuss in "The Goodbye Girl"

Maralynn: I'll be honest, I'd much rather hire a speaker who I like. I'd rather not hire someone that I'm not thrilled about, but if they are the right fit for my group, then I will. The nice part is that the more relatable you are as a human being, the more compelling you are as a speaker. Maybe we have things in common or we have the same sense of humor - those kinds of things matter to me. But, it doesn't have to be me that you're relating to, it could be the CEO who is really into baseball and I learn that a speaker I'm considering attends loads of baseball games in his off-time.

The more human you are, the more people are going to relate to you. You can use that to your advantage. If you are not compelling in any way and have no hobbies or interests, and you don't like chocolate cake or my dog Martini, or slugs, then you're going to have to work on that.

Bonni: Agreed. A slug-less, Martini-less, chocolate cake-less speaker is no speaker of mine. The days of a plain old talking head are over. I don't want an empty shell who lectures about the effects of slugs on the hedgehog population. It's not interesting to me, I need more. I need a person up there. I need a person who everyone wants to talk to and hang out with after. The after-taste has to be awesome.

Shawna: The aftertaste of slugs. Hmm.

Tracey: One thing that worked really well for me when I was trying to help someone choose a speaker was to have them actually have a conversation with that speaker. That way, they could find out whether or not they were going to jive and if there was a likability factor there. They had to have a little bit of a connection. That was really important when wanting to get them to narrow down their list sometimes. It worked really well.

Bonni: There's a process. You talk to me first. You get past the gatekeeper. I'm not going to dive quite as deeply as my clients do into the meat of the content. I want to know you can have a friendly, educated conversation and that you present yourself as intelligent and you have knowledge of your topic. I'd like to know that you can respond to weird questions on the fly and you don't speak robotically. Only then do we get on the phone with the client and have a more in-depth conversation, but I have to make sure you are not an idiot first, because then I'm an idiot for recommending you.

Shawna: Exactly. In my prospecting, I have an amazing sales assistant who prospects for me and casts a really wide net. As soon as a conversation starts and the prospect shows interest in me as a speaker, I want to take over and start building the relationship. Have a conversation. I don't ever want my assistant to book me before I've had a conversation with someone. We establish a relationship that is based on more than just a transaction.

That's what builds trust and leads to re-bookings and referrals.

By forming a relationship, I also might be able to upsell better. Also, what I've found is a planner is far more likely to share their budget with me if I have an honest, human conversation with them.

Tracey: Last year when we were looking at Jana Stanfield for SPINCon, she and I had a very long conversation via Zoom, and found out we grew up in the same area of the country, we were about the same age, we had very similar experiences, and that was the initial part that sealed it for me.

Then she said, "Tell me more about your group and what they're looking for or what you're looking for." Once we started talking about that, she got it. Then, she told me right before the conference that she has never customized a presentation as much as she did for us. Which, again, blew me away and she just nailed it so much on the head, it was incredible, but that was after two or three conversations between the two of us. It was awesome.

Shawna: She made her conversation with you group-centric, rather than Jana-centric. It wasn't me, me, me. She was so smart in saying, "Tell me about your group, what do they want?" She was able to customize it and knock it out of the park. Before you get on the phone with a potential client, Google them. Go to Facebook, go to LinkedIn. Find something you have in common to form the basics of that relationship before you try to sell them a transaction.

Maralynn: Two things: One, I think building a bond is extremely important because I would much rather recommend friends before strangers. If you can become friends and build a relationship, that planner is going to evangelize for you. You're going to have an army of people who are going to tell other people about you.

Two, I heard something interesting that was more sales-related, but I thought it could be used in some fashion if you were having a bit of trouble relating to your audience. Maybe you're a more cerebral speaker and connecting is a challenge. I was fascinated to learn that there were sales people doing this and I thought it would work really well for speakers too...take an improv class. Learn to think on your feet and how to react to people in different ways that are more engaging.

Those are two possibilities. As a bonus, I feel compelled to say chocolate cake and also Martini the Wonderdog.

Shawna: Always appropriate to insert those two into conversation.

Bonni: I've actually created sales meetings where we've brought in an improv pro to teach people how to comfortably communicate on the fly. When you get on the phone with us, as planners, try to know your room a little bit. I'm always the same. I'm always super casual, super comfortable talking to people and you don't ever have to be corporate-y with me. Know your room before you even get into the room.

If I get on the phone with someone and I'm being me, and they're being super corporate, I have to modify my conversation to fit them and that's always a weird thing for me. I always wish that people would let their guard down a little bit, but also when you're talking to a planner, whether she is me or a serious grown-up person, try to mirror them a little bit. Ask the planner what the clients are like.

Some of my clients are like me, but some of my clients will want you to go back to your corporate self. I'll tell you, I promise, but go ahead and ask your planner. I say look, when you talk to the head of marketing they are going to be more like me, but when we get the head of sales, he is super corporate and you need to be a little more like that. The ability to fit yourself into all of these little cubbies is a great quality in a speaker. You are going to get on stage and you need to read that room and decide if you need to modify things a bit to make everyone in the room more comfy.

Maralynn: I've attended a few sessions with speakers who do not know how to read the room at all and it's memorable, but for all the wrong reasons.

Tracey: Exactly.

Bonni: (ahem) Shaquille O' Neal (cough). On another note, I've had speakers who sit in on the meeting the day before their presentation and go and rewrite it completely based on who their audience is. That's somebody I'm hiring again.

Shawna: How can a speaker be likable after the event? How can they make themselves memorable, what kind of thank you do you like to receive, if at all? Let's talk about that.

Bonni: I like a large gift of extreme monetary value. Something I can pawn, if necessary.

Maralynn: My gift of choice is puppies.

Bonni: Other than that, share your slides, engage after the fact, follow the company you just spoke for on social media. Follow them on LinkedIn and engage in conversation with them. You can continue to be a resource and a part of the brain trust of that organization. Tie yourself in with them, the next thing you know, maybe you're a consultant! I can't count the number of speakers who have gone on to become consultants for my clients because they have such a long-term engaging message. These opportunities exist, and you won't know if you don't get in there and engage. Share your slides. Don't be greedy.

Tracey: While I do agree with that, Bonni, a lot of times, and I can see this for the speaker side that in most cases, I think the speaker is going to move on. I would rather see them engage prior to the event. Where you engage with them and find out what are some of their questions, what are their stress points, what things keep them up at night, that kind of thing. Have that discussion whether it's through social media, LinkedIn, whatever. It makes you look approachable and you might actually have an answer for them, which is why they want to hear from you in the first place.

Maralynn: I have seen quite a few ways that speakers have engaged. Some, like Tracey said, just drop off immediately. There are others I've had who say, "Leave me your business card and I will send you blah de blah." The problem is, unless you're lucky enough to have an assistant that you can shove a pile of business cards at, you have to follow up on your own between your many gigs and it can take such a long time for the attendee to receive the item you offered them.

One speaker recently said during her session, “If anyone would like to connect with me, text to blah, blah, blah right now and there will be always be an option to stop if you decide to opt out.” So boom, whoever wanted to connect did it right then and received a confirmation back. They knew they were opted into communications with said speaker and that they would receive periodic messages. This was a great way to stay connected and it was immediate. The speaker could catch as many people as possible right there in that moment, after they had just experienced how amazing she was.

Bonni: But know your audience. I do a lot of customer events for my clients so the last thing they want to see is you advertising yourself at an event. It's a very challenging atmosphere when you are with your client's clients. You have to be very careful about how much advertising of your own stuff you do and that's when that after-the-fact stuff we discussed above can work if my client's clients are also potential clients for you.

I have said 'clients' way too many times. You know who I mean--those people you want to hire you. They may be in the audience, but selling from the stage might not be appropriate. Joining them on LinkedIn and engaging after-the-fact can be pretty valuable.

Shawna: It all comes down to asking the planner what's appropriate and what's not, I think. I did want to share one other tip that I've used to be likable and memorable after a gig. I just, whenever I have a block of time, I look and see what crazy holiday it is that day. National Doughnut Day for example. I sent out emails to, I don't know, maybe 20 past clients who I wanted to just keep in touch with. All I did was, in the subject line, I put their name with a bunch of exclamation points, so it would say, 'David!!!!!'

Who's not going to open that? In the body of the email I said, "Happy Doughnut Day!" I put a picture of a doughnut, but that was all I said. No pitch. I think I heard back from every single one and I got a couple of leads from that, which was fantastic just to touch base and have them be like, "Oh my gosh, I was meaning to reach out to you."

I agree with Tracey, most of that work does need to come up front with being likable, but I think there is something to be said about keeping in touch without it being too much work for the speaker, as Maralynn mentioned, or getting too ingrained, because we don't have time for that, but keeping in touch to be likable and remind them you're out there.

Bonni: That reach out with absolutely no ulterior motive is brilliant. Just saying 'hey we're friends now. Here's a virtual doughnut.' I love that. I love that human connection you've created.

Shawna: A virtual doughnut, what's not to like?

Tracey: What I would appreciate would be being able to sign up for their blog or their thoughts. I subscribe to Seth Godin's emails and I get one every day. Some days I read it, some days I don't, but it's there. Most of the time I love whatever he has to say. Again, it's not too much time for the speaker because the emails are already going out, and it's not too much time for me because I have a choice whether to read it or not. I like that part of it. I feel somewhat connected.

Shawna: Too bad, I hear he's kind of a weenie in person. Total hearsay.

Bonni: What a bummer.

Tracey: Yeah, really.

TOP TAKEAWAYS

1. Planners secretly prefer to hire speakers they like. Humanize yourself by sharing personal details online in your marketing, and in your conversation with the planner.
2. Before you get on the phone with a potential client, Google them. Go to Facebook, go to LinkedIn. Find something that you have in common to form the basis of that relationship before you try to sell them a transaction.
3. Ask the planner what their desired outcome is. Make it about them, their event, and their audience, not you-you-you.

4. Consider taking an improv class.
5. Ask the planner if it's OK to market your tips, blog, books, or anything else from the stage BEFORE you do it.
6. Engage with the organization on-line before and after the meeting to become part of their brain-trust.

   BONUS TIP: A slug-less, Martini-less, chocolate cake-less speaker is no speaker of ours, so be mindful of that. Oh, and puppies are always a solid client gift choice.

Chapter Six: Smart Questions to Ask

"Come on pal, tell me something I don't know..."
- Michael Douglas in "Wall Street"

Shawna: After building rapport with the planner I say, "I know this is an uncomfortable question for you, but would you be able to share your budget for this with me?" I am shocked at how many actually disclose their budget. You just have to ask.

Bonni: I will tell you what my budget is. Any weird back-and-forth where someone is at an information disadvantage is uncomfortable for me. But remember to ask the other questions that go with it like, "Does that include my travel and hotel? Are you interested in me doing a book signing? Are you buying books, or am I selling books?" I buy a lot of books, which can be more valuable than the fee to the speaker if they are trying to boost book sales. Ask those questions.

Maralynn: Besides the obvious question as to whether there will be chocolate cake at the event, there's something you can do that's kinda weird, but simple. Let's say you're going to get beyond the planner and talk to the client, like Bonni mentioned. Try, "This may sound unconventional, but if we were all at Thanksgiving Dinner together, what topics would they like and not like to talk about?" Are they the aunt who is sweet as pie or the aunt who drops f-bombs? Work on learning a few things from the planner about the client that you'll be speaking to. It shouldn't be too difficult if you've already built a rapport with the planner...which you'd better!

Tracey: I've had several amazing speakers who I've hired in the past and oftentimes it's a question of how much more will you do. I had one speaker who attended a hockey game with us because he was a hockey star. I've had others who have been able to do little snippets for our video and other kinds...Jana Stanfield, again, comes to mind as a rock star in this regard.

The one thing I've learned, more than anything is, if you don't ask, you don't get. That's the key, to be sure and ask for whatever you want. Sometimes you can come back later, after the client has booked you and say, "Hey, would you be interested in doing such and such?"

Shawna: I have been on both the planner and the speaker sides now, and I want to urge speakers: do not negotiate your fee down unless you ask for something in return. Smart things that you can ask for, there's a myriad, a ton of things you can ask for. It just depends on what's valuable to you. Do you want referrals to their many planner friends? Do you want video? Do you want the ability to have a table in their exhibit hall? What's important to you? Don't negotiate down without asking for something to compensate you for that value because I believe it decreases your value in the eyes of the planner if you roll over too easily.

Bonni: That's true. Know your value. Know that we judge you sometimes by what your fee is. We expect more from a $50,000 speaker than one who charges $1,000. Yeah, if you drop your fee, ask for something else in return. I will share video with you, if we have it, edited and raw video of your presentation. I will send you what we are sending out to the attendees after the fact, but I'll also send it to you raw in case you want to edit it yourself.

Maralynn: For negotiation purposes, I think it makes a lot of sense for speakers to come up with a concessions list. Maybe you can't decrease your fee, but you can have a list of 12 different things to cherry-pick from during your conversation with the planner to say, "But, I can do this or this...or I can bring you chocolate cake." Have a list of things that you can use rather than trying to pull something out of your butt during the conversation. You definitely, like Shawna said, appear weak in some sense if you don't have your ammo ready. I know it sounds weird because this isn't "The Art of War" or anything.

Someone gave me a piece of advice once that isn't necessarily speaker-related, but I think it'll illustrate my point. If somebody asks you to get together so they can pick your brain and you're happy to do it, don't do it for absolutely free. Say something like, "Buy me lunch and I'll be happy to let you pick my brain." It subtly changes the dynamic and it elevates you in some sense. They may only buy you an eight-dollar sandwich, but at the same time, they're providing something for what you are going to give them. Having an easy-to-reference list of items that add to your worth is in the same spirit.

Tracey: I have had many-a-time that speakers have chosen to go first class. I don't mind you flying first class, but if I don't get to fly first class, you don't get fly first class. I would much prefer to have a speaker tell me that they have a flat fee for travel and make it whatever they need. If you insist on going first class, fine, tell me it's a thousand dollars, it's fifteen hundred dollars, whatever it is, if that's your fee for travel, that's it.

You cover your own transfers to the airport and back. I don't have to pay three hundred dollars for some luxury car to come pick you up in the morning. I don't care if you are flying first class, as long as you get there. I am looking at it this way. You fly all the time. You probably have enough miles you can get yourself upgraded. Why should I have to pay for that? From a budget standpoint, I don't have that kind of money, ever. I don't care what kind of budget we might have for our meeting, but we don't have money for that.

Shawna: I also agree with the flat fee because it allows the planner to know exactly what it's going to cost. There are no surprises and there's no second check that has to be cut afterward. There are no receipts. I like that as both a speaker and a planner. The flat fee that is predictable, and easy for both sides.

Tracey: And also list it on your website. It's helpful.

Shawna: I don't list it on my website because I don't know if I am speaking in Poughkeepsie or Peru and I do customize it to be really reasonable based on where the meeting is going to be. I don't use it as profit center. That's just one reason why I don't personally list mine and it does change depending on where the gig is, how long I'll be gone, all that stuff.

Tracey: Good point.

Maralynn: At this moment, I feel strangely compelled to say puppy.

Shawna: You're like Rain Man.

Bonni: I am always going to get a little negative shiver down my spine when a speaker asks for first class. I get it—I always want to travel first class, who doesn't? It's a conversation to have if it is an issue. The words "first class", though, are a diva alarm system going off in my head. I get it- there is no way I'm flying to Asia in coach- but Newark to Buffalo? That is the kind of thing you have to either incorporate into your fee and, as we discussed before. I'd rather you incorporated travel and expenses into your fee then add it as a travel stipend.

In this case, I'd rather you said, "It's $10,000 for me, all in." You factor in that travel, and then you can walk to the venue, if you want.

Shawna: Another smart question to ask when you talk with us: what do you want your audience to walk away feeling, thinking, or doing differently after this conference? Then incorporate those concepts when you describe your skill set. Also, ask who the previous speakers were – that'll give you an idea of their budget. Better yet, Google last year's speakers before you get on the phone with the planner.

TOP TAKEAWAYS

1. Ask the planner what their budget is (but know that they're probably low-balling you...). Confirm whether that includes travel, books, or other add-ons you may have.
2. Work on learning a few things from the planner about the client that you'll be speaking to.
3. During the negotiation phase, if you don't ask, you don't get. That's the key, to be sure and ask for what you want. Ask for concessions if they ask you to lower your fee. Alternately, offer add-ons to try to keep your fee intact.
4. Ask what the planner's goals are for the conference. Mirror those words back to the planner when you describe what you can do for them.

BONUS TIP: "Will there will be chocolate cake at the event?" should be in your top five questions.

Chapter Seven:

Getting Planners to Respond

"Well, what am I supposed to do? You won't answer my calls, you change your number. I mean, I'm not gonna be ignored."
- Glenn Close in "Fatal Attraction"

Shawna: Let's start with the phone. Ladies, are there any instances where a speaker cold calls you and you would return that call?

Tracey: I just got one recently for SPINCon. I'm not sure how he found me, but for some reason I answered the call. I rarely answer the phone. But I did that day, so he kind of jumped in, he said, "I got your information because I understand you guys need a speaker for

SPINCon..." and he knew. He had done his research, he knew about our event, and so at first, I'm just kind of like, "Ugh. Okay, fine, whatever." And then he mentioned our event, and that he knew who we were and who our members were. So then, my ears pricked up. And I'm thinking, so what do you talk about? And we already booked our guy, but I just said, "What do you talk about?" So, we talked for several minutes, and he would probably be a good person for us to have sometime in the future. I told him, "We've already got our line-up for this year, but show me some information and I'll look at it for next year." So, it was a good call in the end.

Maralynn: I have to be honest, I don't answer my business line anymore. I rarely even answer my cell phone unless it's a number that I recognize, because I get so flippin' many spam calls.

Tracey: Right.

Maralynn: I just wait to filter through voicemails later. Unfortunately, when you call me and leave me a voicemail, it's not compelling enough. I don't necessarily have the time to return those calls. I prefer email, because it's right in front of my face in my inbox. Send me a link, don't send me giant attachments. Send me a link to your YouTube channel and send me some highlights. Highlight just a few things, don't say, "Here's all my work!" Show me a great bit that intrigues me and makes me want to know more about you. That's my preference.

Shawna: To Tracey's point, you have to do your research.

Maralynn: Yes.

Shawna: I get so many solicitations still, and I haven't been a planner for six or seven years now. And I still get so many solicitations from people who haven't done their research, or who send a generic blast, the spray-and-pray technique. And I can't imagine that's successful for anybody.

Tracey: Alright. So in prior months this year, I did get an email from a gal who said that we knew somebody in common, and that person had recommended that I talk to her about her speaking at our conference. Well first of all, that's a f*cking lie. And she had also sent me her book that I did not ask for. And she's like, so check out my book -- and she's been hounding me about her book, so I flipped through it and I was just kind of like, no. I wrote back and told her, "I'm sorry, but this is not something we would look into." I mean, I was very blunt with her.

Bonni: I got a call from someone who wanted to speak at SPINCon and went on and on and on and on. I'm just going to add some more 'ons' just so you all suffer the way I suffered. And she wanted to talk to Tracey or Shawna, and I didn't give her your contact information because she was so incredibly boring, and I couldn't imagine sitting through her speaking at SPINCon. Much like Shaq, she was filled with trite commentary. On the other hand, I do like getting a book. I like getting a book in the mail- it's like getting a puppy. I might just read it.

But, I'm also with Maralynn. Don't call me on the phone. Please. The chances of me needing you and your story right now are so minimal, and if I don't need you and your story right now, I'm up to my neck in some other story.

So do exactly what Maralynn said, send me that email with some links and some interesting stuff, and I will file it away. I have learned not to overly respond to those emails, because then you get sucked into the vortex, into the sales funnel. And you can't get out. So I have a file, I'm paying attention. But even if I write back thank you, that's it. I don't want the conversation to go on for an eternity.

Shawna: Like Bonni, I do like receiving the occasional book in the mail, but I prefer when someone asks first. But, here's something not to do...I got an unsolicited book in the mail from someone, and a week later she emailed me and said, "Have you read my book yet?"

Bonni: Pressure!

Shawna: And I responded, "Thanks for sending it, I put it on the pile." Because I was not awaiting this random book in the mail with baited breath, nor did I know it was coming, nor did I know anything about her. But, I did say I would take a look at it, and when it came time to take a look at it, she had buried in the pages of the book a note to me. Probably to test and see if

I really read her effing book! I thought that's, you know...

Bonni: Cold, that's just cold.

Shawna: Don't remind me within a week that I've failed to read your book in a timely manner, and then don't shame me by including a note hidden within its pages!

Bonni: If you want me to really read your book, bury it in that chocolate cake we have discussed. I'll find it. But it's not homework- we don't want more pressure!

Maralynn: Save the shotgun approach for your dating apps, ok? Because whether it's a generic approach and you haven't done any research or like Tracey mentioned, you're cleverly misrepresenting yourself, we're gonna figure it out. We're gonna figure out that we don't know you or our colleague doesn't know you. Don't get cute. Even if you ARE cute, don't get cute. Because it's going to turn us off before you've even had a chance to tell us what you're all about.

Tracey: Or turn us on.

Maralynn: Same with overly eager people. You can turn me off just by nagging the crap out of me. Because I don't want that experience, and I don't want my client to have that experience.

Bonni: Yeah, if you try to scam me on that first call and tell me that someone recommended you, remember, we talk to each other. We know each other, we'll say, "Hey, I heard you recommended Joe Schmo?" And if you get called out as a liar, you've now closed this whole circle. And we will talk about you behind your back and laugh.

Shawna: And your name shall live on in infamy. But let's talk about email a little bit more, because we've established the phone is not a good idea. Even though I constantly hear at speaker conferences people saying, "You've got to pick up the phone!" No, don't pick up the phone!! We're not gonna answer it. And we're not gonna call you back. And you've annoyed us. That leaves a couple of other methods. So email we've already talked about, what's a good subject line that would get your attention?

Bonni: 'I have cake.'

Shawna: I've heard that the name of your event in the subject line is a good attention getter, because as planners, we're attuned to respond to something that's related to our event. Would that at least get you to look at it?

Tracey: Yes.

Bonni: Yes.

Maralynn: Yes.

Tracey: Yes, I think if they've done their research and can speak to the event. If it's something fun, I can't imagine what it would be but say, SPINCon, and...

Maralynn: Cake.

Tracey: Craziness, or cake. Or something like that. And I might open that, just to see, "Who is this? And why are they bothering me?" But, I would probably read through it. And something else that was said earlier, a link to YouTube or something like that, if you can actually embed that video in your email, not just the link. If you can embed it, then that's even better. Then I don't have to go to some other website, it takes longer. But if you can embed that in your email, then that's even better because you've now made it easy for me to see you. And if that video clip is tied to the subject line and how you can make my conference even better, then I'm gonna pay more attention. I might actually write you back.

Bonni: Yeah. Don't send me a link to another site, because that worries me from a stranger.

Tracey: Yeah.

Bonni: You may go into the, you know, "I'm a recently widowed Nigerian princess" folder, just because it's scary.

Tracey: Yeah.

Shawna: I find it interesting that you actually have a folder like that and you save those emails for what, future use?

Bonni: You know I do. I put them all on Facebook, along with my bizarre friend requests.

Shawna: Okay...Tracey, you brought up a really good point. We've talked about the phone and we've talked about email, now I want to talk about video email. This is one of the things that I tell anybody in my sales audiences: to pursue video email which is exactly what Tracey just mentioned. That you would pay attention to it and you're likely to respond to it. So ladies, Bonni and Maralynn, have you received a video email yet and would that intrigue you? If it's embedded, you don't have to click anywhere else, and they have your name maybe on a whiteboard that they're holding up and it says "Hi, Bonni!" Would you be intrigued enough to open it?

Maralynn: It depends, if they're holding up today's newspaper and saying, "Please send help", I may not. I have not yet received a video email. So Shawna, if you want to send me one, that'd be super cool. But I like that idea and I like potentially personalizing it. You could have something about what you're able to offer, but maybe throw in a quick, "Hey Maralynn, I love chocolate cake and puppies too! I'd love to talk to you more about SPINCon, and there's a video below that'll give you an idea of how I may be able to help you equate chocolate cake with relaxation, and foot massages, and not having to do any work!" I'd be all over that in a heartbeat.

Bonni: Those are all my favorite things. But yeah, I haven't received one either. I would find that compelling, to have a personalized video email, absolutely. But you'd have to find a way to make it eye-catching at the beginning, like you said. Hold up a whiteboard with a picture of chocolate cake or that says, "Hi Bonni!" or dangle a dollar or...you know. Something in front of me that might-

Shawna: I thought your stripper days were over, Bonni.

Bonni: Not by choice. No one's showing up.

Shawna: Yeah, video email is in its infancy, and it's got a really high open rate right now because people are still intrigued, and they're not annoyed with it yet. So yes, I do recommend that they go to the dollar store and get a simple whiteboard and write the name of the person, otherwise it just looks like you generically recorded and you're spraying-and-praying by sending the same video email out to a thousand people. The key is in personalizing it like Bonni and Maralynn said, and talking about the event and showing that you've done your research. And talk about the person a little bit.

Maralynn: Jump on that bandwagon people, video email is the new black! It's not gonna be new for long.

Shawna: By the time this book comes out, video email's gonna be so 1982. It's gonna be like a fax machine. Speaking of which, let's talk about what's old and potentially new again. So, for a long time, nobody sent mail because it was not sustainable and so forth. Now, I miss mail. I don't know what you guys think about mail, but if you get something hand-written in the mail, what do you think about that now?

Bonni: I love to get mail that's not a bill...a hand-written anything. I'm gonna read it. If you write something to me, I am going to read it, and I am going to save your card, and I'm going to remember that you wrote to me. I think it's very old school and Victorian and cool and it makes me want to sip tea and chat with you.

Maralynn: If you think that maybe a portion of your book pertains to me, take the time to print out a few pages. Send me that and a $5 Starbucks gift card and say, "I thought you could check out a few pages from my book I think might apply to your conference while you enjoy a nice cup of coffee!"

Bonni: Maralynn, will you be my marketing person? That's very clever!

Shawna: Maralynn, can I buy some of that lemon poppyseed bread with that Starbucks gift card? Does it have to be coffee?

Maralynn: It can be cake, it can be coffee, it can be nuts, it can be whatever Starbucks has to offer. I like the idea of creating a virtual space. I think it may be too much to say, "Hey, how would you like to have a video call over coffee?" because then I have to go to Starbucks, get my coffee, come back and get on a video call. But if there's something that you'd like to compel me to read, keep it to a few pages because my attention span and time are both short...let's just keep that in mind. This would be a way to at least introduce yourself, show me a little bit of what you've got, and it's a conversation starter.

Shawna: I like virtual coffee! I also just heard of a hotelier who invited a planner to virtual happy hour. The thing is, if they send you a gift card, you're at least going to get back to that person and say, "Hey, that was neat."

Maralynn: I'd at least get back to them and say thanks. I'm not a savage.

Shawna: So we now know Maralynn's attention can be bought for $5!

Let's talk about LinkedIn connection requests. How can a speaker get you to accept their connection request on LinkedIn?

Tracey: I have connected with quite a few speakers, because when I was in the speakers bureau business, it was kind of important. But what I do not like is when they immediately pounce on me with a message saying, "Thought I would tell you about my speaking abilities, and blah blah blah blah blah." It's like, "Okay stop. Just stop it." And I've actually said that to somebody, "I'm not interested right now, I just wanted to connect with you." So I'm a bitch, aren't I?

Bonni: You're an awesome bitch. You are the queen bitch. You know, Shawna is always evangelizing on the importance of sending a message with that invite. Don't just blindly send me a generic friend request on LinkedIn, it's not a Facebook friend request—a connection request on LinkedIn is business. Send a message, send something that tells me why we should know each other. I do not socialize on LinkedIn, so if I don't know you, and I don't see a valid connection, I'm not going to accept. If I do accept however, do not reach out to my connections. Don't use my sandbox as your sandbox, and stop touching all my stuff. There's something really icky about you using my virtual rolodex as a collection tool for contacts.

Maralynn: One of the things I prefer is, if you already have connections with other planners who know you as a speaker, go on LinkedIn and see if they are connected to anyone who you are interested in getting to know. If you've had a successful interaction with Bonni, look on LinkedIn to see if Bonni and I are connected. If we are, send a quick message to Bonni and say, "Hey Bonni, would you mind introducing me to Maralynn? And if you found value in what I provided for you, I would greatly appreciate a good word and the connection." Something as simple as that would be a lot more effective than me getting a random request...I see he knows Bonni and Tracey and Shawna...I guess I'll accept. Those connections don't hold as much weight, and I'm not going to think about it afterwards. I'm not even gonna remember your name. You're just gonna be one of a thousand people I've connected to on LinkedIn.

Tracey: Totally agree with you on that, Maralynn, because I actually spent time when I was unemployed beefing up my connections, so I had reached a thousand one summer. I don't know all these people personally, I know them through the industry. And we have met at a conference, or they've just connected with me, and if they're in the meetings industry I will usually accept their connection. Just because, who knows if I might need them someday. I could reach out, I could go in and look and see are there any planners in the San Jose area, for example, that I know. And I would reach out to those people saying, "What do you recommend for blah blah blah blah blah?" But I've had people actually reach out to me and say, "Do you know so and so? Because you're connected on LinkedIn." And I'm like, "I don't really know them personally, but you're welcome to say you found that connection through me." So that it's not freaking them out that there's just some random, weird equation that connected them. But I'm not always gonna recommend somebody, I'm not always gonna say yes I'll be happy to introduce you. Because if I don't know that person, no.

Bonni: I try to limit how many invitations I accept or even send out, because I really try to keep that list to be *my* actual network as opposed to *a* network. This is my network, I know these people, and like Maralynn and Tracey both said, if you see somebody who you want to meet in my circle, and I know you and we know each other, then I'm happy to introduce you. But I try not to have extraneous people I don't have a connection with on there.

Shawna: That train left the station for me a long time ago. I'm more of a LinkedIn ho at this point.

So many nameless, faceless connections in the dark. But, unlike Bonni, I always say to anybody, feel free to use my name if it's helpful, but I think most planners are gonna behave like Bonni, where they protect their network and don't accept just any connection. So, getting introduced to Bonni, as Maralynn suggested, is really the best way to make a new connection. Ask the planner, "May I copy you on this and use your name?" would be another option, because Bonni may not want to drop everything and send an email to introduce me to someone, but she may be okay if I copy her, so she knows what's being said.

Bonni: I love to introduce people to each other, when it makes sense. I love to connect the right people to one another. So yeah, definitely ask me. People can always say no.

Shawna: Bonni, you hit on something fantastic, and that is: Ask me. Because I am always telling sales people, they don't ask us--their clients--for favors. And once we've crossed the barrier from salesperson and client into friendship, I will absolutely do favors. But if you don't ask, you don't get. I'm not often going to think to go out of my way to do something to help you. I might not come up with that idea on my own, but if you ask, I will absolutely help you if you've served me well. If we've crossed over into a friendship, and you ask me, would you mind introducing me to three of your planner friends? Boom, I'd introduce you. Easy-peasy.

Bonni: I'm the same, I want to help. If you're somebody who's been impactful to me in any old way, if I think you're funny or nice or interesting, or I've seen you or heard you or read your stuff. Or we just have a good connection. Then I want to do nice things for you. Maybe you've brought me cake in the past.

Shawna: Or nuts.

Bonni: Or nuts. I do want to help you, but it may not pop into my head, "What would be a nice thing for me to do for Tracey?" It may not occur to me. But if you point it out to me, yep, I'm gonna do it.

Shawna: So ask more. You know when the rapport is built, and if you've nailed it, ask for what you want afterward.

TOP TAKEAWAYS

1. Planners rarely answer the phone these days. A brief email is preferred, without huge attachments or a long sales pitch. Include a link to your demo reel. A good subject line is simply the name of their event.
2. Sending a book to the planner is a good idea, but it's best to ask permission first.
3. Video email is trending right now. If you try it, personalize the beginning of the recording with a customized dry-erase board showing the planner's name.
4. Hand-written notes in the mail are always appreciated and very memorable.
5. Use my name or my connections to reach out to others, but asking first is preferred.
6. Feel free to ask us for favors once we've crossed over from client to friend.

BONUS TIP: Don't spray-and-pray and don't suck us into your sales funnel...we no likey! We like cake.

Chapter Eight:

What to Say When We Do Connect

"Damn glad to meet you."
-Tim Matheson in "Animal House"

Shawna: What can we suggest to speakers to say to us when we do accept their connection request, or respond to the email, or—egads—we pick up the phone?!

Tracey: I'll start! Do your research, and if you have done your research then you will know what kind of meetings I plan. So if I plan sales meetings, but you talk about something that's not related to sales, then move on to the next person. If you speak about sales and you're very good at it, then you might say, "I see you have a sales meeting coming up next February, I would love to chat about how we might work together to make it the most spectacular event you've ever had." Now, you got my attention.

Maralynn: Whenever you can approach things by showing you want to do whatever you can to help others, it comes across more honest and genuine. A couple of years back at SPINCon, Shawna had us exchange business cards with a stranger across the room and then on the way back, hand that card to another stranger. For the rest of the conference, we had to search for the random person and ask, "What can I do to make your life easier?" That's huge for us, because especially as planners, we're the ones who always take care of everything. We're the one planning family events, details, everything. Nobody ever says that to us! It's so refreshing to have someone say it to me...it might even render me speechless for at least five seconds.

Bonni: No way. No one's gonna render any of us speechless for five seconds. There's this magical story I have about this one time when a speaker called me to sell herself and it was clear that it was not a good fit. She then introduced me to somebody else, another speaker who she knew from just being in the industry. It wasn't like her best friend ever, but she'd heard her speak, and she thought she was great, and she thought she might be a good fit for me. And she introduced me. And that was heaven. That was chocolate cake in a basket of puppies right there. And a rare thing, because nobody's helping us do our job. And if you're helping us do our job, in a selfless way like that, you're my best friend. I mean, present company excluded.

Shawna: I think one mistake some speakers make is when they do connect with us, they start asking us a bunch of questions about the event when it's too soon. We don't want to have a 60-minute conversation with you. Keep it brief until the time comes we're ready to talk about a specific event. That also shows you didn't do your research. I mean, know the basics about the event.

Bonni: We may not know anything about our event yet. We might not even know what it's called yet. And we may have 15 other events going on that you might be a fit for, that you're excluding yourself from. But most of the time, if I don't have a keynote speaker for my event yet, there's not much I can tell you about it. Because a lot of my event's gonna be wrapped around who my keynote is.

Maralynn: Like Shawna said, peppering me with 30 questions? That's not how I want to spend my time. Maybe I want to be on the phone with you for five minutes to find out a little something and ask a couple of questions. You find out a little something during that conversation you might be able to use, and then follow up with a tiny little video clip that might apply to what we were talking about. Or like Bonni said, you may not be a fit for this conference, but you have a resource that might be great for me. I'm gonna remember you because of it. And I'm also not going to be super annoyed by you, and you're not gonna get thrown on the pile of annoying people who probably-

Bonni: The annoying pile.

Shawna: So we've been talking about what to say when you make that very first connection, like you're trying to get yourself known to a planner. Now, let's say the planner has responded positively and says, "Yes, I would like to learn more about you as a speaker for this particular event." That kind of changes the dynamic a little bit. How does that change what they should be saying, or what they should be asking? And I'll start this by saying, ask about the goals of the conference. Ask smart questions before you jump into a pitch.

Maralynn: One question that I try to ask all of my clients is, "What do you want people to walk away with? What's the aftertaste you want in their mouth when they leave your conference?" That's the most important part. In my planning, what I say could be something as simple as, "I really don't think we should cut the food and beverage budget by half because no matter how awesome your content is, attendees are going to walk away from your conference bitching about the food." I find it's a really effective question, because it gets to the point. Sometimes asking what the "goals" are makes people think in bullet points...like business goals, which is not taking into account the humans in the room. What's the feeling you want people to take back with them and how can I help you get there?

Bonni: That was brilliant. That's exactly right. And it always comes down to what the goals are for the meeting. The real questions: "What are we *really* talking about here? What's the challenge we're working with? What are we trying to fix? Are we trying to make evangelists out of your clients, or are we trying to get your salespeople to play nicely together? Are we preparing your company for sale or are we trying to rebrand?" There's always that main goal of a meeting that gets advertised, and there's always that sub-goal, which Maralynn described perfectly. How do you want people to feel at the end of this conference? And those are the messages I'm gonna be charged with trying to get across. So those are the quiet little things that aren't being advertised. So good on you, Maralynn.

Shawna: Good on both of you.

Maralynn: And this may be a third-date conversation, but without getting mired down in the bottom of the toilet bowl, I ask clients sometimes, "What's worked in the past? Tell me some things that have not worked or tell me about a speaker who went over like a lead balloon. I want to know what kinds of things to avoid. Most likely, those are not things I would do, but I would love to learn from your experiences." And as a planner, we have plenty of negative experiences that have happened in the past, and we're happy to tell you about them.

Shawna: Yes. And we're going to tell you about many of them, in a later chapter of this book.

Tracey: Stay tuned.

Maralynn: And to go back to a previous statement that Shawna made, these things you might be doing that we suggest you avoid may live on in infamy. You may also end up in a book like this. So, be careful.

Bonni: You may have already seen yourself in this book!

Shawna: Unfortunately, the people I've already referenced in this book will not see themselves in these caricatures.

Bonni: They never do.

Tracey: No.

Bonni: Back to the original question, about what kind of questions to ask. Go a little farther in the demographics than age and sex. Get titles and departments and find out who that audience really is. Are these people who get together every year, or are these strangers to one another? What is it that brings them all together? Because those questions are a little bit more than what the demographic is. Try to get a little bit more meat out of the planner.

Tracey: I would say also to try to figure out the emotion behind people who are attending. I have had some meetings where the company was in a threat situation, where people were gonna lose their jobs because of a merger, and so there's fear. And you could smell it in that particular meeting. There've been other ones where, times are changing, the economy is changing, and people are just unaware, or they don't know what's my job gonna look like, two or three years, five years from now? And so there's that curiosity or again, a little bit of fear about that. And how can the speaker help them through that and help them get past that particular emotion. There could also be happiness and celebration and let's just have a party kind of thing. With cake, of course.

Maralynn: Of course.

Shawna: That's a beautiful point, to not be tone deaf. Because if they're in fear of their jobs, you don't want to come in as a motivational speaker. And I think we know a general idea of that type of speaker who's totally tone deaf. And it goes back to what Maralynn said in an earlier chapter about being able to read the room. But you should know the basics of that room long before you get on stage. And then once you're on stage, be able to pivot accordingly, but you should know way ahead of time, as Tracey said, whether there's fear, or whether there's uncertainty, or whether they're celebrating. And lastly, Bonni said earlier, get more meat.

Speaking of which, I would like to wish all of you a happy National Fried Chicken Day, which is today.

Tracey: It is today! I saw that, I thought of you.

Shawna: You thought of me?

Tracey: Because you love weird holidays.

Shawna: Oh, okay. I thought it was because I really like fried chicken.

Maralynn: Remember that place where we all had fried chicken in New Orleans? That was so good.

Shawna: Yes. The best fried chicken in New Orleans, but we digress.

Maralynn: We do digress.

Tracey: I like fried chicken and I cannot lie!

Maralynn: And if you want to know where you can find the best fried chicken in New Orleans, then you can just contact us via...email, LinkedIn, Instagram, Facebook. We'll give it to you.

Tracey: Perhaps in a little video email.

Bonni: That's gonna be my next marketing tactic. I know where the best fried chicken is...

TOP TAKEAWAYS

1. Want to make a planner speechless? Ask what you can do to make their life easier.
2. If you're not a good fit for a particular conference, you can endear yourself to the planner by recommending someone who is. You'll be remembered, liked, and possibly referred for your selflessness.
3. Great question to ask a planner: what's the feeling that you want people to take back with them and how can I help you get there?
4. Building our connection is going to take a little bit of time...don't come at us like a spider monkey with your sales agenda.

BONUS TIP: Don't get thrown into the 'annoying' pile and don't forget about the aftertaste! Oh, and we know where the best NOLA fried chicken is.

Section Two:

At the Gig

"Alright, Mr. DeMille, I'm ready for my closeup."
- Gloria Swanson in "Sunset Boulevard"

Chapter Nine:

On Site

"Watch me dazzle like a diamond in the rough."
- Jemaine Clement in "Moana"

Shawna: So, let's start out with talking about how speakers can really knock it out of the park when they're at the gig. And this isn't just about, "Hey, you're doing a great job speaking in full sentences!", it's how can they really set themselves apart?

Maralynn: I saw a very memorable speaker a while back. She spoke, but she was also the emcee for the program. With every speaker who got up on stage after her, she found a way to tie their messages together with thoughts about the conference and things that even she spoke about. She tied things up after every speaker so it kind of book-ended things. And it was done really well, for the entire conference.

She also went out of her way to meet virtually all of the attendees at the conference. For her to be able to say, at the cocktail reception, "I was talking to Bonni about puppies and chocolate cake, and we came to the amazing conclusion that those things rule!" and then connect that to an idea or a thought within her messaging, had BIG impact. Little things like referring to attendees by name or remembering something personal about them can really help take you to a different level. Bring that all back to your message and you've got something amazing.

Bonni: The hardest part of building a conference is keeping it cohesive. So if you can be part of closing that loop, if you can help facilitate creating one full cohesive message out of the mess of the past three days as an emcee or as a capstone speaker...anything you can do to help facilitate that very elusive process is always going to be welcome. So again, go to the cocktail parties, the other presentations;

find what needs to be added in on stage to be part of that closed loop. That's always going to be popular and appreciated.

Tracey: I've had a few speakers, and I was blown away by what they did but also so appreciative because they really and truly brought it home. And that was, they learned the jargon of the group. And so in both cases, it was an industry, and so they had their own jargon and their own acronyms. And it was amazing how these speakers incorporated them into their message. And it brought the house down. Everyone suddenly was tuned in to that speaker, because that speaker now understands me and my life. And that was what was so important.

And another one kind of referred back to his notes and he says, "Okay, I'm looking back at my notes about you guys and you blah blah blah blah blah." And again, it tied that group together. They were now listening to him because he understood them and he took the time to listen and take notes. So, it was very important.

Bonni: And pulling out your notes is not necessarily a bad thing. We're human. We want you to be an actual person up there, so I think it's great that they pulled out their notes. There's nothing wrong with that.

Maralynn: And the impact that you make on stage is huge. Not necessarily for just that moment, but beyond. You're in front of a planner who can potentially connect you to tons of other planners. If they're a member of SPIN, they have the potential to rave about you to 2,500 other planners. But the entire room is potential business for you, right? I mean, you could be speaking in front of hundreds or thousands of people who could potentially hire you or tell other people about you. And there's no better way to evangelize than to get other people to do it for you. And if you can make an impact on their brain and or their heart, they will absolutely do that for you. I mean, I've done it.

Whether it's an experience at a hotel or with a person, whatever it might be, I've found myself talking about it when I never intended to talk about it. Because it impacted me in such a profound way.

Tracey: Another way speakers can make an impact like that is to get the audience involved in their presentation. So, the interactivity of it. And if you can get them to expose themselves a little bit, and then bring that point back. Geez. Not...okay.

Bonni: Just to clarify, do not expose yourself on stage.

Tracey: I'm trying! I mean to reveal things about themselves, to reveal something about their...is that worse?

Shawna: My inner 12-year-old boy is tee-heeing. 'Reveal.' Haha!

Tracey: She's so exposed. Okay. So, to share something about themselves. Okay. Time. Go to Maralynn!

Maralynn: To Tracey's point, something as simple as making yourself more human to the audience is going to get them to connect with you better. Humor works great. If you can get people to laugh and evoke some emotion, it'll stick with them longer. And I think to be able to show you're a vulnerable human being will help them connect to whatever material you have, because they may have something in common with you.

Shawna: I love that, and also what we were talking about earlier with not delivering a cookie-cutter presentation. That is so old school to me, that you give exactly the same presentation 100 times a year, and the same presentation that you gave a year ago, or five, or ten, or God forbid 20 years ago, and you're still giving it today? I think that's cheating the audience.

Tracey: And we've all seen speakers like that. In fact, we had one recently at SPINCon whose every gesture was choreographed, and every joke had a pause for laughter, and you could tell that this speaker was rehearsed within an inch of her life. She could have been anywhere, and I think it's the biggest disconnect you can have today with an audience. Whether your audience is 20,000 or whether it's 20, you've got to do something to make that human connection to show you did research, to show you're not just anywhere, you're with *my* group.

Bonni: It goes back to something we discussed before, which is you really want to be having a conversation with the group. If you are up there, and you are speaking *with* the group as opposed to speaking *at* the group, and you're being interactive with the audience, then you're halfway there. You want to feel like you're in a conversation, even if you're the only one talking. But be careful about those practiced moves and those practiced pregnant pauses and those trite little nuggets of wisdom you throw out there. Try to talk as if you're chatting with someone you know, but you don't swear around...like your mom.

Shawna: Let's talk about trends on stage. So, Tracey mentioned earlier: talking to your audience, asking questions, engaging with the audience. And we've talked about incorporating your message, we've talked about not being tone deaf. One trend I'm seeing is shorter presentations. And I'm not talking about the TED talks, but are you getting demand from your clients to have shorter and shorter presentations to cram more stuff into the day?

Bonni: I am. I fight it and I do advise against trying to overstuff your agenda. People think if they're going to be together, they have to take advantage of every second. I try to remind my speakers and my client that some of the stuff can be done by email and webinar prior to or after a conference, but you don't want to shortchange it. On the other hand, a two-hour keynote is going to make me want to kill myself.

Shawna: Yes. As it should.

Tracey: As it should. But, I personally don't have the attention span for anything more than 30-40 minutes. And so, I really don't want a keynote speaker to go on for that long unless they have extremely compelling information to share.

Shawna: Every keynote speaker thinks that they have extremely compelling information to share.

Tracey: No, the truth is they don't.

Shawna: We know this to be true, from the other side of the lectern.

Bonni: But they don't know it.

Maralynn: I've learned quite a bit watching the way Shawna speaks. She keeps the audience engaged. It might be, "Everybody stand up and we do jumping jacks for 30 seconds!", or something less strenuous. One of my favorite ones, I remember asking you this specifically, was how you get them back when they start to talk amongst themselves. And maybe you can speak more about that, unless it's a trade secret, then you can kill me so I won't ever disclose it.

Shawna: I will have to kill everybody who reads the book. Which is logistically challenging for me, and I'm very busy. That said, I simply give a low SHHHHHH into my microphone. I used to travel with a cowbell to get attention back after table discussions, but I found out nothing works better than the shush. It's ingrained into us from Kindergarten.

Shawna: I just went to an amazing conference that was crowdsourced, called Haute Dokimazo. So this conference, we broke into crowdsourced topics, and one of them was on how to deliver a meeting in the ways that people learn today, with shortened attention spans. And one of the things that came up was chunking a presentation. In seven- to ten-minute, bite-sized mind nuggets, if you will, speaking of chicken and it's National Fried Chicken Day. But, chunking your presentation, and every seven to ten minutes, pivoting and delivering your content in a different way. Whether that means showing a video, to break up the monotony. Or having a conversation in the audience, with the audience or at people's tables, or whatnot. And then bringing it back. But yeah, because I have A.D.D., I like to put things into more digestible content chunks for my audience so that it is more memorable, more impactful, and more digestible. All those things that you want as a speaker.

Bonni: Look, a bunny!

Shawna: Look, a squirrel!

Tracey: I totally agree with you and heard a really good speaker a couple of years ago talk about that very thing, and what he did was sit through a talk show. So Jay Leno, or some of the newer shows now. And he literally wrote down, minute 000, and timed everything and knew exactly how many seconds each section of the show lasted, including the commercials. And so if you watch, I'm really aware of it in the morning news shows, that they will give you the headlines for about three to five minutes, and then they go to, I swear to God, at least seven minutes worth of commercial. I mean, you can go have breakfast, you can come back, you can do your workout.

It's ridiculous, before you hear another segment of news. But that's what we're used to. And so he was talking about that, it made perfect sense, because our brain doesn't stay forever listening to someone, we check out on a word, you say squirrel and now I'm looking out the window going, is there, I wonder where that squirrel went. And then you come back. So you've got to build your presentations where you can do that kind of thing, and I think speakers really need to be aware of that. Even though we have limits to our attention span, they really need to break it up so that it's exciting to us in a manner that we're already used to seeing. So, like a talk show.

Shawna: I don't know a single keynote speaker these days who would be riveting enough to hold my attention just talking for an hour. Yet, I would bet 80% of the speakers reading this book are saying to themselves, "I could."

Bonni: I think one of the ways to put this is re-engagement. You just have to keep re-engaging the audience over and over and over and over again. You're not gonna grab their attention when you walk in and hold it for 45 minutes. You have to continually re-establish that connection.

Maralynn: And contrary to what you might think, throwing things at the audience is not a good way to re-engage them. Unless it's puppies!

Tracey: No, you don't want to throw puppies!

Bonni: Don't throw puppies. Why do I have to keep telling you this?

Maralynn: But typically it's not good to beat the audience with stuff to keep their attention. So you gotta figure it out on stage, maybe some interpretive dance, I don't know.

Tracey: We're back to interpretive dance. It's always-

Shawna: Did we ever leave interpretive dance?

Bonni: Interpretive dance is always the answer. As Tracey is demonstrating for us right now.

Tracey: I also think that you can take a lesson from Facebook and...which I'm sad to report that I'm somewhat addicted to. And so, I get my little bits of information in 10-30 seconds. Again and again and again and again and again. And if a video goes more than a minute and a half, I'm like, "Oh, do I really want to watch that?" And I will make a decision based on how long that damn video is, but if it's really cute and does have puppies in it, I will watch it. So there.

Bonni: It's not just Facebook, everything we look at now is in tiny digestible pieces. And we are trained for it, we're being trained every day by everything we watch and everything we read to shorten our attention span more and more. And it applies to your audience. We are no longer capable of digesting too much in one sitting unless it's filled with music or flashing lights...or puppies.

Shawna: One of the cool things that Tracey is incorporating into SPINCon is quiet time required by every speaker. Think back to kindergarten again. Quiet time for the last three to five minutes. If you have an hour, the last three to five minutes are quiet time, because the way the brain is bombarded today, and the way that, especially meeting planners, are constantly having to shift gears, we don't have time to just sit, and digest, and reflect. I think that's really cool. I know the readers are thinking right now, I only have 45 minutes and you want me to give up five of it? Think about just trying it and having people reflect as one of your methods as chunking their speech, having them write down something. I'm really excited to see that in action this year.

Tracey: Me too, the thing that got me in the article I read said the brain has been working, working, working, listening, paying attention, and taking in all of this information. And it literally needs to rest. So, the five minutes of quiet time is just rest for the brain. And the brain will take all of that information and create synapses if it needs to, or whatever, but it will put all of that information into the database and say, "Okay, now we know this." And then it can move on. And I love that idea, my brain is such a powerful tool and I really need to be able to give it time to do its job. So, I'm excited about trying that too.

Shawna: Although five minutes right now sounds like an eternity, I will be interested to see how it feels when I'm part of an audience, because I know on stage it would also feel like an eternity, so maybe start smaller and see how it goes, and see what the planner thinks and what the audience thinks. And then, after that quiet time, come back with your killer closing story or your killer recap.

Bonni: I love the idea. It is terrifying to think about five minutes of quiet, but SPINCon is such a safe zone for things like that, where we are allowed to try and fail. That's where we're trying things out. But the idea of time to digest is incredibly appealing to me. None of us really have down time. None of us really have time after we've learned something to absorb it. We walk out of a meeting room, out of a session, and right into another one. Or right into networking, or right into something.

Tracey: The phone.

Bonni: Or your phone, exactly. There isn't time to just think on it and reflect. I really love the idea. I think five minutes is an eternity though.

Shawna: And if you're a speaker and you're thinking about trying this, this is very new and trendy. But give them time to think about it, and make action steps. Action steps are going to make your information more memorable than the other speakers who don't do this. And wouldn't you rather, in the end, be the most memorable speaker from the conference?

Bonni: And don't be afraid to say, "I'm trying something new as a speaker." Don't be afraid to, again, you're human. We want you be human, we love it when you're human. And say something like, "I read about this or I saw this, let's try this together." It's a bonding moment as well.

Tracey: Yeah. I would love to see a speaker try it within their presentation where even if they took a minute, and just said, "I'm gonna let this fall on you, and maybe I'm trying something new or whatever." I love that idea too. "But, let's just take a minute and you write down your notes, or you think about what we just talked about, or what just happened on stage, and then we'll get back to it." And just have that transition period.

Bonni: It just reminds me of a presentation I saw at a conference I managed. One of our board members owns a marketing company that works with life sciences and his company produced a video. And it was all about breast cancer and the BRCA gene, and it was very moving. It was a video with a survivor, but not everyone in the video was a survivor. And at the end, that's what he did. And I guess I didn't realize it until just now, but he gave us a few minutes to just sit with that, and it made it all the more impactful. Because if we went from, 'and then they died', to, 'let's grab some coffee and snacks', you lose that moment. We all just sat with ourselves, and it was really far, far more impactful than it would have been if we had to move on to lunch or anything.

Tracey: We just had a webinar, oddly enough, where the presenter gave us time in the webinar to write down our thoughts. And she said we're gonna take so much time, and she told us how many minutes, and she actually had a timer. And she said, I want you to write down your thoughts about this thing, and then we're gonna move on to the next thing. And we did this four or five times, and when she first said that I'm thinking, “Oh, no. You're not going to dead space on a webinar.” But she did it, and it worked out so well because I actually did write down my thoughts on this thing, and it was so impactful for her point she was making because my preconceived notions about that changed as she talked. And it was like, I didn't even know I thought that way. So it was biases and prejudices, and thoughts I didn't even know I had, and it was really amazing how it worked well in that webinar. So, it can be done in a keynote or a session or whatever. If it can be done in a webinar, it can be done anywhere.

Shawna: It can be done anywhere.

Bonni: If you’re doing that, my first thought was, if you're gonna tell people you're giving them time to write stuff down, let them know it's just for them.

Shawna: Yeah.

Bonni: As opposed to, this is part of an exercise and we're all gonna be talking about it later. It takes away the pressure of having to write something brilliant, and it allows people to be more authentic with what they're putting down. If it's going to be part of the session, let them know. If it's not, if it's really just reflective time, then let them know in advance that that's what it's going to be.

Tracey: I'm much more open if I'm not sharing.

Shawna: Yes. And I might learn best, or process best by doodling unicorns and baked beans. And that's for me to doodle as I process whatever I just heard, whereas somebody else might just make a list, and somebody else might just sit there and meditate on what they just heard. It just all depends on how you learn.

Tracey: True.

Shawna: Okay ladies, before we close up this section, I want to talk about: To PowerPoint, or Not to PowerPoint? And if you do PowerPoint, what are the trends speakers should be aware of?

Bonni: PowerPoint should not be your presentation. You are your presentation. PowerPoint should be the parsley on your plate.

Shawna: Amen sister!

Bonni: That one impactful photo and one word, or a snippet of video, is a beautiful use for a keynote PowerPoint. I don't want to see a chart, I don't want to see a million words. I don't want you to read to me. These are probably all things you've heard before a thousand times, but if you haven't stopped, then a thousand and one is okay by me. That's the exclamation point; your PowerPoint slides, your keynote slides, your video. It's about what you have to say. You can always do handouts later, if you must. Shawna's brilliant at this. One excellent picture that's funny or moving or somehow directs the mood. That's what your slides are for. Your slides are not for information. Information can be distributed; I don't want a tiny chart on a screen. Jesus God, don't show me a chart. I will cut you.

Tracey: I'll give you the f*cking knife!! There are times when a chart is appropriate. In scientific sessions, of course. Or something that's really pertinent. However, some speakers seem to think we need to see the whole chart at once. We do not. We need to see your point at once. So, yeah. Zero in on that one point. If this particular part of the market is doing this, tell me about that. If another part of the market is doing something else, tell me about that. I don't need to see them together. You would have it as a chart, ordinarily, but break it apart. And chunk it out, as we've talked before. Salient points people can truly understand. And they're gonna pick up on it much better if it's delivered one at a time as opposed to all together.

Shawna: If your chart makes more than one point, it's too complex these days. Rethink it.

Maralynn: I have a few educational seminars that I provide, and this is really simplistic but something that makes a big impact is the pictures of cats, dogs, and small children making funny faces that I incorporate into my slides. If you can get them to laugh while you're trying to make a point, they will remember more of what you just talked about. I've used pictures as the punchline to a setup. There are a lot of different ways, but the more you can sort of catch them off guard without actually using nude photos of yourself, is impactful. It will stay with people. The nudes probably for the wrong reason so I don't recommend it, but there are a lot of things you can do. Maybe you have a cute dog, maybe you have a cute grandchild. It could be anything and you can use it and incorporate it into your presentation to make a point.

And what Bonni already said, detailed slides are not the goal. We've finally gotten past the point of, "Can I have the entire slide deck, so I can read and know everything you just told us?" Your real value is providing information verbally while playing off of images and photos, so they can't get all the good stuff in your brain from the tiny writing on your presentation slides. They engage with you, and you engage back with them. You show more value that way, and you're also not super-freaking boring. Because I'm one of those people who will actually doze off.

Shawna: I hear from speakers all the time who don't want to share their slide deck because it's their intellectual property. And to Tracey or Bonni's point, if your intellectual property is found within those slides, you are doing a disservice to your audience. As Bonni said, that should be the parsley on your plate, not the main course. My slide deck is worthless to anybody who wasn't in the audience. Because it is a picture, and no more than five words. I learned that long ago from a friend who's a neurology nerd. No more than five words. And if you can put one word, that's even better. If I have to sit through another presentation with a speaker who puts a quote on a slide, and then reads it to me, I'm gonna go get Bonni, and she and I will cut you together.

Tracey: And again, I'll provide the knife.

Bonni: Hold my baby, I'm gonna cut you.

Shawna: Hold my beer while I watch!

Bonni: Our clients still want your slides. Some people learn that way. One of my speakers did a little extra work; he took those slides that were just a picture and just one word, and put a sentence or a paragraph next to it in the slides they were distributing. And this is a very well-known speaker and author, a talking head, so if somebody's gonna be stealing intellectual property, they're gonna be stealing his. He's not worried about you taking his information, we have paid X amount of dollars for him to share that information. So you take the slide, you modify it a little bit for distribution, you save it as a PDF so nobody's cutting and pasting it and using it as their own and you share it with the audience. That's part of your value as a speaker, to share your knowledge IS your value as a speaker. And if you're not willing to share it, then you've undermined your own value. But, do modify your slides to reference back what you were speaking about for people who learn that way.

Tracey: Something else about that is, some of us are visual learners, and some of us are auditory learners, and I'm a little bit of both. But, I tend to remember what I saw more than what I heard, because I don't really listen that carefully.

Shawna: Shocking. News flash.

Tracey: So, I do like the visual part of it as well, so to me having slides, even if it's pictures, is awesome. Because that kind of ties it together, and I remember it better.

Bonni: And don't ask us to hand out physical copies of your slides.

Shawna: That is so 1992.

Bonni: I have given my attendees things to write on to take their own notes, they don't need your slides to take their notes. Please email them to me so I can share them with the attendees or give them to them on a memory stick, so they have them if they want them. But, the idea of printing out 500 copies of your slides to hand out and then throw away immediately after is terrible. In addition to being unbelievably wasteful, it smacks of a little bit of self-importance.

Shawna: So another trend is speakers ditching their slides altogether and just coming up and presenting. There's a fair amount of Slide Shaming from speakers who no longer believe in using slides. Now, to Tracey's point, I also am a visual learner, and so I like the visual addition to someone who's speaking. Like we said, it shouldn't replace, the speaker should still need to be present to interpret what the slides are referencing, but I do still like a tasty set of slides. As long as it's done well. What are your thoughts, ladies?

Tracey: Yes.

Bonni: I've had a few speakers now who have ditched the slides. It takes people aback. I don't know if people are ready for it yet. I find it easier to pay attention to someone who's talking if there's nothing for me to read in the background, I get very distracted by written word. Recently, I was watching a show and I couldn't turn off the closed captioning, and I literally couldn't do both. Because I went right to reading, and I had no idea what anybody was saying or doing on the screen. So for me, wordy slides can be distracting in that way.

Shawna: So you will never be a judge in the Academy Awards Foreign Films category?

Bonni: Unlikely. If there are words, it takes away from everything else for me. A written word throws me.

Shawna: So you're an auditory learner.

Tracey: My husband likes closed captioning because he's hard of hearing, and we can't watch a movie together. It's really hard for me, I'm sitting there reading the lines as they're going along and I'm not watching what's up on the screen, and I have to physically force myself to ignore the written word and look at the video.

Shawna: This goes back to speakers who put their whole freaking speech on their slides. Don't do it.

Maralynn: I think this has probably been discussed ad nauseam, and I think most planners allow for it... But in the past I've been in situations where out of the blue the presenter's says, "Oh by the way, I have a Mac." or "Here's my presentation!" when they were supposed to give it to me 30 days prior. And all of a sudden, I'm scrambling backstage with the AV guys trying to figure out how to get the damn thing up on the screen in three minutes. You can't spring that crap on us at the last minute. If we ask for format, or we ask for something specific or we say we need a flash drive and we're gonna plug it into a PC, that's the way it's gonna work. If you draw outside the lines, we'll figure out a way to make it work, but we're gonna secretly hate you.

Bonni: Not secretly. I'm not gonna secretly hate you, I'm just gonna hate you right out there in public. Shawna does a great thing on her website, a page called 'For Planners'. Everything you need-her photos, her bio, her audio-visual requirements are all right there. If you work on a Mac, bring a flipping dongle. I have one, I have a dongle. Not everybody does-- I see it all the time at other people's meetings. It should be part of your kit. And don't get cute on your audio-visual needs. Here's what we have, you can ask for anything you want, but understand that there's a budget in place and that there's a process in place, and sometimes you can't have twelve Phil Donahues with mics walking through the audience even though that's what you really want.

Tracey: Be respectful. Just like Bonni just said, you've got to understand. And also, the AV at the meeting may not be what you're used to, so you've got to be respectful of that as well. So, just because you think everybody's got the same kind of AV technology at their meetings, they don't. Just be aware.

Shawna: And if something goes wrong with the AV as a speaker, I know, because I was a former planner, never blame the planner from the stage. Never blame the AV person from the stage. You just make nice about it and move on. Or recover, or punt. But, you don't want to make an enemy of the AV guy, trust me. That AV guy will haunt you. He probably knows what room you're staying in. And you really don't want to make an enemy of the planner by throwing the planner under the bus. More on that in Speaker Horror Stories, the final chapter.

Bonni: One of the ways you can become more relatable to your audience is by rolling with the power outage, or the slide not moving forward, or the mic going out. Nothing says diva like somebody saying, "Umm, next slide please...NEXT SLIDE!" in the middle of the presentation. Just roll with things.

TOP TAKEAWAYS

1. Go to the cocktail parties, the other presentations; find what needs to be added in on stage. Reference attendees by name from the stage. Tie in other speakers' messages. That's always going to be popular and appreciated.
2. Don't be too wordy with your slides. You are your presentation. Your slides are parsley.
3. Be flexible with your audio visual, and come prepared if you have a Mac.
4. Be generous with you materials. None of us plan to steal it from you, and it is a big part of your value.
5. Be a resource. There is no one we value more.

BONUS TIP: Do not expose yourself on stage, and interpretive dance is always the answer.

Chapter 10:

Extra Stuff You Can Do to Add Value

"Second prize is a set of steak knives.
Third prize is you're fired."
- Alec Baldwin in "Glengarry Glen Ross"

Tracey: One speaker we hired to come to our event and speak was a professional athlete. He was a hockey player. He signed hockey pucks for everyone in the audience. We didn't ask him to do that. I mean, we did ask him to do it, but we didn't pay him extra to do that. That was really a nice bonus. I mean, he sat there in his hotel room and just signed every single one of them. That was beautiful. Then, I had another who's a celebrity who has written some books. He signed 400 books after he spoke, for another big conference. Things like that, they just add so much value to what speakers can bring to the event.

Bonni: On the book signing note, I almost always hire authors, and I almost always want to have a book signing. Of course, that's valuable for the speaker as well, you want to sell your books. But yes, please stay and sign your books. That's huge. Signing hockey pucks, really awesome.

Tracey: Yeah and very appreciated.

Maralynn: Yeah, I think being creative with that stuff is important, because you want to differentiate yourself. Offering something outside of the traditional meet and greet...maybe 30 minutes with an audience member, could be great. Maybe it's a short coaching session before everything starts. Something you can offer that the client could potentially use as a drawing prize would be appreciated. Giving something as extra added value, when it's only costing you 20 or 30 minutes, could be extremely valuable and could elevate your reputation as people discuss you moving forward.

Shawna: I've seen where planners have auctioned off things like that from a speaker, to raise money for their association or charity. Very cool if a speaker offers it as a perk, especially to a nonprofit.

One of the things as a speaker I always offer now is to do a promo video beforehand. I think that's becoming common and almost expected now. So you may as well offer it up as a perk. But not a lot of speakers offer to do a follow-up video. And I think this is just bonus exposure for the speaker, if you can do a follow-up video or a follow-up series of maybe three videos that are each three minutes long. Just re-emphasizing your key points, re-emphasizing what they learned, or challenging them with new action steps. It's just more face time for you, and they send it out on your behalf. You can put a little promo or a call-to-action at the end of the video for, "Hey subscribe to my list," or tips, so you get that added value. So, I think it's a huge win-

win. And I know planners love that extra value-add.

Bonni: I had a great speaker last year, who's a well-known podcaster in this really niche market. So everyone in our audience listens to his podcasts. He did the coolest thing; he stayed an extra day, and we gave him a little room, and he brought some equipment with him. And he gave people the opportunity to record their own podcast with him as the interviewer. So, it was a really cool extra bonus. All he really did was the recording. He didn't necessarily make it his. When it was relevant, and with the ok of the guest, he used some of them on his own show. But for the most part, he just gave them this podcast of their own that they could then link to their website, or put on LinkedIn as this little interview people could share as part of their own marketing.

Bonni: And it was great for him, because he gained additional audience each time somebody listened to any of the podcasts. Because he'd say, "Hi, this is, ..." and he got new subscribers. And people loved it. That was a good one.

Tracey: One other thing that we often did a lot of with the speakers bureau, was ask for meet-and-greets. And so that's another thing you can offer as a speaker, either before or after.

Shawna: I still remember the most expensive speaker I ever booked. And Tracey was the speakers bureau rep who helped me book it! And that was Alan Greenspan back in 2008. We paid him $200,000 plus a private jet, which was $73,000. And Tracey helped us get him to come backstage an hour beforehand, for a VVIP meet-and-greet with 50 people. We brought our photographer back there. Mr. Greenspan signed books, and those 50 top, top people were able to get their picture taken with him. We got a company to sponsor that, and it ended up being a nice moneymaker for the conference, the sponsor got great exposure to the top people, and it was exciting for all those VIPs. You may not be Alan Greenspan, but a private meet-and-greet can still be a perk you can offer, and something the planner might be able to get sponsored.

Bonni: And Tracey got a new car that year.

Tracey: I did not get full commission off of that one, couldn't co-broker. Shawna's client did send me a fee, though, but still, I was happy to help.

Shawna: While we're still on the subject of sponsorships, planners love if you are able to help them to schmooze their top sponsors or exhibitors. For example, ask the meeting planner if there is a sponsor or two they'd really like you to give a shout out to from the stage. You can go further and tell a success story that involves the sponsor, or call them up to do something with you on stage. Or is there an exhibitor who would love you to do a book signing in their booth? With the planner's permission, you could even approach exhibitors and ask them if they'd like to sponsor your book signing by buying a bunch of your books, which you sign in their booth.

Bonni: We've also had speakers who will allow themselves to be recorded by our team, and give little testimonials about the conference, which is also helpful for next year. Especially some of these really good speakers who are able to, off the cuff, give a quick blurb about what a great meeting it is, and how much they've enjoyed it, and how everybody's so brilliant and good-looking, and tall, and there's cake and everything. And everyone's happy. But that's a nice little something you can use for next year's advertising.

Maralynn: The speaker I mentioned in an earlier chapter could remember names like nobody's business. I was really impressed, because throughout the conference, she remembered my name and she remembered something specific about me. It made me feel special, and also it made the conference more memorable. I mean, I know not everybody can do that, but her memory was amazing.

Bonni: Yeah, if you have that gift, that you can remember people and remember details. I remember stupid generic stuff about people all the time, and it always serves me well when I run into somebody at a conference. It's always something like, "You're allergic to strawberries!" But I remember going to see a speaker in a concert hall. I bought tickets; it wasn't a meeting. He's somebody that I've gone to see a number of times because I just love him. Last year when I went to see him, when I lined up for the little book signing, he's like, "You wore that awesome poncho last year." I was like a 12-year-old. Yeah. I was so excited he remembered me. And so when you give people that little gift of saying, "You're memorable," that's something you can't really buy. So if you have that gift, use it.

Shawna: And if you don't have it, fake it by writing stuff down about people so you can act like you remembered later! As far as other things you can do to add value, see if they have an internal magazine or a blog. Offer to write a follow-up...this is just extra exposure for you, and an extra touchpoint that makes you more memorable as a speaker. Or, if you're a podcaster, can you do a podcast dedicated to their organization, interviewing their people? And then lastly, we talked about it before, but share your dang slides! You can customize the header and the footer for extra visibility, such as, "Subscribe to my tips. Here's the web address." Don't just deliver your value at the conference and leave. How can you stretch it out for your own good, as well as your audience's? It's a win-win, I'm telling you.

Bonni: We had the executive editor of Wired Magazine speak at a conference for us a few years ago. He gave everyone in the audience a subscription to the magazine, which was really cool. They are kind of a techy group, and probably half of them they had subscriptions. But he sent ahead the latest issue so that we could distribute copies at the meeting. And in addition to autographing his book, he would sign the magazine. He gave us a simple login code where you could have a free one-year subscription to his magazine. And now he has an additional 500 subscribers that he might not have had before.

Bonni: That's cool...anything you have access to that you can give away without it really costing you anything, winds up being valuable for everybody. Because if you have a magazine, or a podcast, or a blog, you want those subscribers. It's worth giving stuff away for you to have access to them, but then people are grateful for that generosity. And if you're generous, it makes the planner look good. You make us look good and we're going to love you.

Shawna: We've all been in the audience when somebody comes up after the speaker and delivers their outro. And speakers, if you don't have an outro, get an outro, not just an intro, but an outro. That way you have some control over what's said after you walk off stage. And we've all been in the audience when somebody comes up, "Wasn't Phil great? And as a special gift, Phil's going to give you all, a new car! Woo!"

Bonni: You get a car, and you get a car.

Shawna: Yeah, so in your outro, have someone else be the giver of the gift, and then you'll get extra applause, an extra touchpoint from someone else on stage. What can you give away for a lasting impression?

Bonni: And yeah, as Shawna said, if somebody else offers it, it looks a little less self-serving. And we are all self-serving, but it's always better to let someone else make that offer on your behalf, if you can get away with it.

Shawna: Ladies, anything else speakers can do to go the extra mile?

Bonni: Yeah. I think anytime you can offer to emcee something, head a panel, join a panel. Try to avoid monetizing every single thing. Try to look at some of what you give as an investment.

Tracey: Another thing you can do, especially if you're just getting started in the speaking business, is offer to do another session. If you're doing a keynote, and can do a breakout session, that really, really will add value for your planner, as well as the client. So, that's a good thing to offer as well.

TOP TAKEAWAYS

1. Do you have something of value you can offer the audience? Or something the group can auction off to raise money? Offering that to the planner gets you bonus points!
2. Offer to do a promo video to promote yourself and the conference. After the conference, offer a video to reinforce the points you made. Include a call to action at the end of the video, such as, "Sign up for my tips here."

3. If you're a podcaster, leverage that to add extra value to the planner and the meeting by interviewing key figures in the organization before, after, or even at the event.
4. If you're an established speaker, offer a VIP meet-and-greet to the planner.
5. Ask the planner how you can help them deliver value to their top sponsors.
6. Ask the planner if, before you leave, they'd like you to do a video to promote the conference for next year.

BONUS TIP: Unlike belly buttons, you should have both an intro AND an outro.

Section Three:

After the Gig

"Where we go from there is a choice I leave to you."
- Keanu Reeves in "The Matrix"

Chapter 11:

Following Up After the Gig

"Did we just become best friends?"
- Will Ferrell in "Step Brothers"

Shawna: Ladies. What's the best way for a speaker to follow up with you and say thanks after the gig? Besides chocolate. Duh.

Bonni: I think a handwritten note is everything, now more than ever. I'm really bad at it myself. You can send a note to our clients or to the stakeholder of the meeting. Send a little something personal that reminds you of them, if you are able. I talked about coffee with someone, and he sent me a pound of coffee and a nice mug. I try to pay attention to what my clients are saying, and send something small with a handwritten note reminiscent of that. I had a client who said that she loved lavender, and I sent this little tiny gift basket of lavender seeds and lotions, and a handwritten note. People remember that forever.

Tracey: You have to be careful with gifts, because a lot of corporations are banning those now. So the note, the handwritten note is probably the biggest thing you could do. And if you can do a little $10 thing, what Bonni said, that's awesome. But the handwritten note is probably the most important.

Bonni: Yeah, don't send a big thing, because that puts the onus on the gift receiver to then follow-up, and it can become an issue. Don't send me a new car unless you really want to, and then go ahead. But you know, a $10 gift, yeah.

Shawna: What about a bag of unmarked bills, or maybe perhaps a large US Savings Bond?

Bonni: Bonds are good, untraceable, very nice. Foreign currency. Big, giant gift cards, yeah, that kind of thing.

Maralynn: Bitcoin, Amazon gift cards, those are all really good too. I think depending on how busy you are as a speaker, carrying those handwritten notes with you when you're on the road, and writing the note before you leave that gig, could be valuable. Then, you don't have to look back and remember what you did a week ago if you've done two other gigs since then, and there's something personal included in that note. "I really enjoyed our conversation about tequila." or whatever it was. You have it right in front of you, because I don't know about anybody else, but my brain is like Swiss cheese. So, I forget crap all the time. It's really nice to be able to get it done right away, even if you just put it in a spot where you mail it when you get home.

Tracey: In addition to that, I will caution you, if you're speaking internationally, to wait till you get home to mail that. Especially if the planner or the client is US-based. Because I've had mail not ever make it, never showed up when I mailed it from Europe. They go on strike all the time. Another thing I would say is, write some thoughts about your experience with that group, send an email to the planner afterwards and say, "Here are some things I really enjoyed about the group," or even recommend another speaker at some point, or somebody you know. But, just a quick little email.

The handwritten card is still important, but the quick email afterwards, when you're on the plane, just compose an email and just say, "It was really nice to meet your group, loved them. Here's what I saw, here's what I understood about them."

Maralynn: Yeah, just some basic reflections, right?

Tracey: Mm-hmm.

Maralynn: It's like, "These are some things I came away with that may be valuable to you for the future."

Bonni: Keep in mind, too; if you're at an international event, make sure you know their gift-giving customs. Especially in Asia, the significance could be something very unintended, you could offend very easily, or send the wrong message. There are a million books, articles and resources online about gift giving in other countries.

Shawna: Something you bring from home I find is always appropriate. Like something traditional, or some small little thing that represents your home state or something like that is always easy, and memorable to the recipient. Unless you're speaking down the street, then it's a little weird.

You don't have to figure out the person. But, that said, the more you can figure out the person, the better. I spoke at a conference, and the guy who hired me, I got to know him at the conference, and he wore crazy socks each day. And I went on his LinkedIn profile to connect with him afterward, and I found out he had a history degree. I went on Amazon, and I found these crazy socks with historical figures...oh, it was the four presidents of Mount Rushmore on the socks. And, I sent him these socks through Amazon.

Now the challenge with that, the mistake I made, was that I sent them as a gift directly from Amazon. And Amazon includes this very forgettable throwaway-able note that says whatever you type on it. But it's easy to miss. And I don't know that he knows who in the heck ever sent him those socks. And I don't want to feel like a jerk by going, "Did you get my gift? What did you think of the socks?" So next time I would have those shipped to me, and then mail them out to him. I know it's an extra step, but I don't know if they were ever appreciated or recognized as being from me. I want credit!

Bonni: Credit is important.

Tracey: One of the best things a speaker can do is to send a note, whether it's an email or a thank you note. Handwritten is preferable. But if it's an email, it would be great to send to the stakeholder of the meeting, to the person who hired you and paid the bill, to tell them how nice it was to work with your planner, and any other people that you dealt with while you were there. You know, just a nice compliment for those people, because they work their tails off for these meetings, and they never get thanked. They'll love you for it.

Bonni: A LinkedIn testimonial is always really valuable to the planner. Because we're in the same boat you are. Especially we independent planners, we are also looking to get rehired and recommended. So, anything like that is always really nice and creates gratitude and strengthens that relationship.

Shawna: And don't forget the power of video. Sending a video email to the stakeholder, talking about how great the meeting was, the audience and the planner. And then sending the planner a testimonial about how great they were to work with, that they can then use to get rehired by the client, or to approach other clients. Rave about just how professional, or on top of things, or what a great attitude, or anything to schmooze the planner. We love that!

Maralynn: As Bonni said, we're all self-serving to a degree. But without being completely self-serving, I think the more you can create a cooperation or a partnership with that planner, the better. I mean, there have to be companies that are contacting you directly, and they may need planning help, and it's extremely helpful for me to have advocates who would recommend me as a planner to others. And as a speaker, you have access to people I may not. And same on my side. I want to be able to refer you to other people if you were really great to work with. So if you can create that partnership, it can be valuable on both sides. And as a planner, I would be extremely grateful for that partnership instead of dealing with speakers as one-offs, you know? Someone I have a bond with is someone I want to work with in the future and I want to see succeed.

Shawna: Maralynn, I think that's a fantastic idea. If you know the planner owns their own business, ask them, "Are you looking for new clients?" Because as a speaker, you may know of an organization that is looking or has just lost their planner. And to be that conduit will make you forever memorable to the planner, and endeared to their heart. Just by making an introduction.

Maralynn: Yeah, if anyone asked me, "Are you looking for new clients?" it'd make my heart all fluttery. Because no one has ever asked that.

Shawna: No one ever.

Bonni: Yeah, that would make my heart go pitter-pat, too. But, also be a resource in whatever way you can. I may have questions about your topic later, that maybe aren't going to bring you a piece of business right now. But, if your subject matter is iguana husbandry and I am trying to mate my iguanas, and I have a question about iguana love, maybe I can call you and ask you about it? Now, that might not mean I'm going to hire you for my next Iguana Fest, but maybe Iguana Palooza next year.

Maralynn: The name of our next book must be Iguana Palooza.

TOP TAKEAWAYS

1. Handwritten thank you notes still hold a lot of value.
2. If you send a gift, it doesn't need to be big. Something that comes from your home state or country, or something you discovered the planner likes - those are always appreciated.

3. Email observations or your takeaways from the conference to the planner. That info can be hugely valuable to us.
4. If you refer a new client to a planner, you win. Everything.

BONUS TIP: We planners love when you rave about us to others...about our looks, our youth, and also about our mad skills. Oh, and if you start an Iguana Palooza, you best send us some free tickets.

Chapter 12:

Getting Rehired by a Planner

"I wish I knew how to quit you."
- Jake Gyllenhaal in "Brokeback Mountain"

Shawna: Let's talk about how a speaker can get rehired for your next conference, or your other conferences?

Bonni: Let us know in what other areas you have expertise. I may not be able to hire you for the same thing, but I have a number of speakers that I have worked with for years, at different conferences. Because I've learned more about them, and about what their area of expertise is. Often, as I said before, I'm hiring you for a little niche kind of area, but then I find out about your expertise in toads as well. And maybe the Annual Toad Fanciers Meeting is coming up. Maybe it's lizards in general. Maybe reptiles.

Tracey: Amphibians.

Bonni: Amphibians in general, yes.

Maralynn: I think when you've booked something with a planner, you've got a great opportunity to create yet another advocate. And, if you are willing to put in the time and build that bond, it could pay off. Obviously, you have to take the planner's preferences in mind. If they don't have time to talk to you, then do not badger them. But when you're on site, take a little time. "Hey, let's grab a quick drink. I'd love to find out more about you." And, at the same time, you can also give that planner an idea of the other things you have to offer. Because I'm sure, like most people, you're multifaceted, and you have other things to offer, besides Iguanas. And this is your chance to create yet another evangelist for your speaking business.

Bonni: Going back to my speaker who offered to record podcasts for people, he did one for me. At the end of the conference, he was going to spend the weekend, because we were in Boston. His wife was going to come in and he was going to spend the weekend. And he said, "If you're still here and you want to do a podcast that you can use for marketing, we could do a quick interview, and we could run it off after your clients leave." And boom, I mean, that was a great gift for me, that was much better than chocolate. Could have done chocolate and the podcast, but, you know, whatever.

Shawna: So with getting rehired, I recommend starting the conversation with the planner, "Where are you off to next?" or "What keeps you busy all year?" Just to have a conversation about what else they work on. And then bring up, as we've talked about, "Oh well, I could possibly be a fit for that," or ask them if you can refer other speakers. "If you tell me about that conference, or tell me what your goals are for next year, I can maybe refer you to some other speakers." That endears you to the planner. They may end up discovering things that you have expertise in that they're not aware of, that you haven't talked about yet. So, ask them what they're working on next and ask if you can be helpful to them or recommend other speakers.

Shawna: And I've developed some really cool relationships where other speakers are great follow-ups for me, or vice-versa, so we refer each other. And so I just referred one of them to come in next year after I spoke this year for one particular client. Planners love that, too, if you can help lighten their load.

Bonni: Don't inundate us with emails looking for more business, please. Emails are not our friends. We get, like I'm sure you do, hundreds of emails every day, and you wind up just clicking to see what you can delete before you even read it. If there is one thing I've learned from Shawna, it's to give my emails a much better subject line, so it's something specific. Make it brief and easily readable, but please don't blast us with too many marketing emails. That can leave a bad taste in our mouths really quickly.

Shawna: Along those same lines, don't add us to your mailing list without our permission.

Bonni: Testify.

Maralynn: Hells yeah. Don't do it.

TOP TAKEAWAYS

1. When you're on site, try to spend some quality time with the planner. "Hey, let's grab a quick drink. I'd love to find out more about you." And, at the same time, you can also give that planner an idea of the other expertise you have to offer.
2. While on-site, ask the planner, "Where are you off to next? Or what keeps you busy all year?" Just to have a conversation about what else they work on. It may give you ideas for other ways you could be involved with the organization.
3. If you're not a good fit for the planner's next meeting, refer speakers that you trust. It builds your relationship with the planner, and builds referral partnerships with other speakers.
4. Don't inundate us with emails asking for gigs, and don't add us to your marketing database without permission.

BONUS TIP: Bonni is obsessed with animal husbandry. She's the one to thank for letting you know that toad expertise could come in handy in your career and that SOMEONE needs to hold an Annual Toad Fanciers Meeting immediately.

Chapter 13:

Getting Referrals

"Say hello to my little friend!"
- Al Pacino in "Scarface"

Shawna: It always amazes me how people don't ask for referrals. Because very often, your planner client isn't going to go, "Oh, you should talk to my planner friend, Becky." you know? But if you ask them, "Do you know of some other planner friends you might be able to introduce me to, and I can take it from there?" or, "May I use your name and copy you on an email to them?" That's also great. But just asking the question, "Who else do you know that I might be of service to, or that

I might be a good fit for?" is important. Because planners, we all know each other. We all talk and refer back and forth. I know what these ladies do and what they look for.

Maralynn: One thing planners are really good at, and I think speakers can do too, is to build yourself a network of speakers who are local to you. Find those people, get to know them, get together for cocktails once a month. Talk smack about whatever's going on! Give yourself the opportunity to bond with these people who are probably dealing with some of the same issues you are. And if you can create your little tribe, kind of like the four of us have, you have opportunities for referrals right there. Because you've got speakers who are in your corner, who want you to succeed just as badly as you want them to succeed.

It doesn't always have to be a planner, right? It can be other speakers. And you want to have your little group of people who you know you can refer to a planner, and know you're giving them a solid speaker who does a great job. Pop in on fellow speakers, if it's possible. Ask them for permission, or watch one of their recorded speaking gigs, so you can get a good feel for what they deliver. Build a little pod of people you know for sure you can refer who will do an amazing job. And they can refer back for you.

Shawna: I love my speaker mastermind group, and my speaker family within NSA. I refer all the time to help a brotha or sista out! Wow. I sound "street." I'm *so* not "street." I'm a middle-aged woman from Minnesota, y'all.

Tracey: [Laughs] I run an organization of a lot of meeting planners. It's called SPIN. And they talk amongst themselves a lot about speakers. We have a private page on Facebook, and we get a lot of discussions about that. And I don't know, maybe I'm just drawn to speakers in general, but over the years when I was in the speakers bureau, and now that I'm with SPIN, we've had speakers, and I've booked speakers. And so I know a lot of them. And there's a handful that I will recommend. So, it's a good idea to try to get to know the planner as much as possible, because we do talk amongst ourselves. And we will recommend speakers to each other.

Maralynn: Or, *not* recommend speakers to each other.

Bonni: This little group of four here are my personal board of directors. Here we are, four people, all in kind of the same world, but we all have completely different skill sets that complement each other. So, if you can find yourself a little board of directors like this, where you have a couple of other speakers who have a complimentary skill set, the opportunities are going to be endless. Because you can create panels together, you can create networks together. If I need a speaker who speaks about sales today, it's very likely I'm going to need a speaker who is talking about marketing tomorrow.

If you're in that same universe of subject matter, but have your own area of expertise there, that's going to be a great group of people who can...you know, you get to really understand each other, and then you can recommend one another. Which to me is more likely than getting a group of planners to recommend you. You're going to get more business I think from one another. Because I do go to my speakers, and say, "Who else is like you, but not you, because you know, I already have you."

Tracey: There are these five prominent speakers who collaborate. I don't remember all five of them, but it's Randy Pennington, Larry Winget, Joe Calloway and two other guys. And they get together and drink Bourbon or something like that, smoke cigars, and they talk about the things that interest them. Which is business, stuff going on in the universe today, things we would all be interested in. And they record these discussions, and they send them out to their client list, and they send them out on Facebook and any social media they can think of. And they have a name for themselves, like the Five something or another, I can't remember what it is. But anyway, they don't speak about the same thing, so they collaborate, and they discuss things based on their own sphere of reality.

Shawna: It's also Mark Sanborn and Scott McKain. They call themselves The Five Friends.

Tracey: Five Friends, yes, okay. So anyway, but it's really fun because you kind of get them in their real environments. You see them just chatting with each other. They just talk about what's going on in the world, and just give out their opinions. So you get a really good sense of who they are. And Larry Winget is just the wildest guy in the world, but he is so funny. And I would consider hiring him, but he's a little bit of a renegade. Anyway, but you get an idea from the Five Friends, you know, and they refer each other, I'm sure.

Bonni: That's their tribe.

Tracey: It is.

Shawna: One last thing is a referral bonus. Let the planner know if you ever think of anyone who might book me, I do this referral program. It doesn't have to be money, but, again, you can't go wrong with large savings bonds or a car. But seriously, maybe an Amazon gift card. To Tracey's point, though, a corporate planner may not be able to accept that. You can also offer to donate to the planner's favorite charity. That always goes over really well. So, a formalized referral program is not a bad thing either.

Bonni: I really love that donate to your favorite charity thing. I think that's a nice follow-up after-the-fact as well. If you get a feel for the person, you can make a donation in their name to something you've found to be important to them. You know, like if they're a dog person, like all of us. Or an iguana person.

Shawna: Here we go with iguanas again.

TOP TAKEAWAYS

1. If you've done a good job for the planner, especially if you have built some rapport, ask them for referrals.
2. Build yourself a mastermind group of fellow speakers if you don't already belong to one. Other speakers are a great source of referrals.
3. Consider creating a referral program to reward those who send you business.

BONUS TIP: Cars as referral bonuses are always a good call. Oh, and Shawna is the most "street" blonde woman from Minnesota that you'll ever meet, and Bonni has a thing for iguanas.

Chapter 14:

Testimonials

"But enough about me, let's talk about you...
what do YOU think of me?"
- Bette Midler in "Beaches"

Shawna: Ladies, what's the best way for speakers to go about getting testimonials from us, from our clients, and from our attendees?

Bonni: My favorite is Shawna's method: grab your phone and ask me right then and there to do a video. Do it while we're there. Ask if you can record me, or write it down, and I will sign it. Please don't ask me to write a letter. I used to write letters all the time. I've run out of time and kindness and all of those things. And I don't write as many letters as I used to. Make it really easy for us. I know that's really selfish. But if you stick a camera or a recorder in my face, I will say nice things about you. And often...I've had people ask me, "I want to write a letter of recommendation for you. What do you want me to focus on?" And that's a really good question. So you might say to me, if you're going to write a letter, "I'm really trying to get into a different field, a different area. And if you could talk a little bit more about my Botany Sales Techniques, that would be really helpful." Then I'll talk about botany.

Shawna: I spoke at an NSA Chapter and Barry Banther, future NSA president was there. And nobody knew he was the future president at the time. But I asked him if he would do a video testimonial for me. And he said, "What do you want more of?" And I thought that was brilliant. I told him I'd love more gigs in finance and automotive, and he customized the testimonial. Just brilliant, and so kind of him.

Normally when I ask people if they'll do a video testimonial, I'll say, "Would you repeat what you just said to me?" Which is also good. Because people come up to you as a speaker all the time if you do a good job, and they say, "Oh, that was great," or, "I love this." That's when I typically say, "Would you repeat that into my phone?"

But back to Barry's great example, going forward, I will now say, "Here's what I'm looking for more of, I'd love if you mention X, or recommend me for this," or, I will ask them, "What's one thing that really stood out, or what surprised you, or what's your number one takeaway?" Just plant those seeds. Because, you put a camera in someone's face and man, a lot of them just freeze up.

Bonni: I get smarter. I don't know if it's pure panic or what. I start using big words and I start making more sense.

Shawna: Bonni is an anomaly.

Bonni: Just walk around with a camera in my face all the time, and I'll say smart things.

Shawna: The video testimonial is so much more relevant today than the written testimonial. Because as a society, we just don't read that much anymore. And also, written testimonials can be easily faked. A video testimonial is harder to fake. It's harder to fake emotion and excitement, and the audience in the background if you catch them while they're on site. It's just so much better than written. So go for video testimonials. I try to never leave a gig without at least two.

Maralynn: What do you do with all of them?

Shawna: I put them on my YouTube channel, and include the link to my channel in every proposal I send. If the person mentions a specific industry, I'll leverage that when I reach out to speak at other events in that industry. I'll include a link of the relevant videos when I reach out to the planner, for instant credibility.

TOP TAKEAWAYS

1. Don't ask a planner to write a testimonial or letter after the event. Get something quick and easy on site, like a video testimonial.
2. When audience members come up to you after you speak, and they say nice things, ask them on the spot if they'd repeat what they just said into your phone on video.
3. Try to never leave a gig without at least two testimonials, preferably video. People don't read or trust written ones as much these days.

BONUS TIP: As grandma always said, "If you don't ask, you don't get." She also said, "If you ever feel sad, just put a little lipstick on," if that's helpful to you.

Chapter 15:

The Final Chapter (and the most fun)...

Divas & Horror Stories

"I don't know how to put this, but I'm kind of a big deal."
- Will Ferrell in "Anchorman: The Legend of Ron Burgundy"

Shawna: Ooh, this one's going to be fun. I have worked with a few diva speakers. Frankly, they are the rarity, and I'd like to believe that most of the time, they don't even know they're being complete divas.

Bonni: Yeah, I have worked with a number of divas, but far more regular, down-to-earth people. My favorite is a doctor who walked in with an entourage, and full makeup. He was quite orange. It was a small meeting, we're talking about 150 people, so to have full makeup in that environment was pretty obvious and strange. We'd been talking for months, so he certainly knew who I was. I hired him. I sent him a giant check. I walked up and I introduced myself and I said, "Hi, I'm Bonni Scepkowski." And he said, "Diet Coke."

And I proceeded to refer to him as 'Diet Coke' for the rest of the meeting, because that's how he introduced himself and that's how I roll. So, with my staff and with my clients, for whom it became a big joke, we referred to him as Diet Coke. "What time's Diet Coke going on?" "Ran into Diet Coke in the elevator." Every interaction showed him as disrespectful and demanding. We were all amused, but not impressed. I would never work with him again.

Shawna: I wonder what it's like to be in his brain, and to be him?

Bonni: I can't even... I can't even imagine. Don't want to know.

Maralynn: I think one of my favorites was a speaker at an analyst meeting I managed for about 600 people. We were in full-swing during the second day of the program, and we had a speaker who was coming in later that afternoon.

About three hours before he was due to arrive, my main hotel contact came over to me and mentioned that he'd gotten a phone call from this speaker's assistant and he was doing his best to accommodate the requests. I said "Well, let's back the truck up. What requests does he have?" And he said, "Well, it's a little bit complicated, but we're working on it." And I said, "No, no, no, no. Tell me what they are." And he said, "Well, he's requested that in the first 30 seconds, as he's coming up onstage, everyone be handed some warm baseball stadium peanuts, and to ensure that there is a scent of popcorn wafting through the room."

Shawna: Wafting! hahaha. Did he actually use the word "wafting?" Because that's impressive. And also awesomely pretentious.

Maralynn: Yes, wafting was definitely the word...that'll stay with me for the rest of my life.

Bonni: [Laughing] Wafting is in all of my riders.

Maralynn: As it should be. So, once I got up off of the floor from laughing, I said, "You know what? I'm going to call his assistant and talk to her about this." And so, what we agreed upon was that there were no peanuts possible. The popcorn machines, that luckily the hotel did have, could not be set in the ballroom quickly enough between speakers. So, they set them up in the corridor and opened the back-of-the-house doors and just fanned freshly popped popcorn smell into the room.

Bonni: Thus the wafting.

Maralynn: Yes. Which was mostly just extremely embarrassing for me, but we did what we could to make it happen. I have to say that was one of the more unique requests that I have gotten from a speaker.

Shawna: I bet he was disappointed that you didn't warm his nuts.

Maralynn: Yeah, I made that real clear up front, that was a deal breaker for me.

Bonni: How very salty of you.

Shawna: My favorite recent one was at SPINCon. For readers who don't know, SPIN is the association I founded, that Tracey currently runs, and Bonni and Maralynn are long-time members. SPINCon is our annual meeting. It is the most casual meeting ever, people are literally encouraged to wear pajamas, yoga pants, and bunny slippers. This is clearly explained to everyone in advance. This diva speaker showed up dressed to the nines, with her film crew in tow. She looked ridiculously out of place. After the event, in the feedback that she gave to us afterward, she scathingly shared how disappointed she was that her video footage was worthless because someone was wearing unicorn pajamas in the audience.

Bonni: As advertised.

Shawna: Yes. As advertised, this meeting was very, very casual, and this speaker did not read what we sent. Shame on her for shaming the meeting planner. Also, as an aside, something that really ticked me off is that she also invited an entourage of her speaker friends to just show up at this closed meeting without registering or even notifying the meeting planner. It caused quite the kerfuffle when one of her uninvited guests was asked to stop partaking of the food and leave - the guest was really rude about it. I have lost respect for the speaker, and I will never, never refer her. I don't care if she can shoot rainbows out her backside. Her behavior was horrid.

Bonni: One of my favorite stories is not really quite a diva thing, just a little irony. I produced a program where the subject matter was working with different generations, so we had three expert speakers: a baby boomer, a gen-Xer, and a millennial. The millennial speaker was going to talk about helicopter parenting and about how her upbringing created that generation's personality type and work style. The overarching theme addressed how to better understand each other and work together. The day before the meeting, she asked, "Could my mom come and watch?" because she hadn't seen her speak before.

Shawna: [Laughing] Shut the front door!

Bonni: The front door is wide open.

Shawna: Truth.

Bonni: I wound up letting her mom sit up in the balcony where our audiovisual crew was working. It was hard to say no, because she had already brought mommy to DC without asking, so she was already onsite. However, no matter how much she begged, we did not allow her mom to sit at the head table and have lunch with her daughter and my clients.

Shawna: Didn't mom pack her own lunch for herself and her daughter?

Bonni: The daughter just assumed that she could have whatever she wanted.

Shawna: Definitely not ironic, haha.

Bonni: Ironic only in an Alanis Morissette sort of way.

Shawna: So, how can speakers ensure they're not being divas onsite? Or in advance of the meeting? What would you really like for them to do?

Bonni: My favorite speakers come in and say, "How can I help make your program successful?" They are low maintenance. They see themselves as part of the management team that's putting this meeting together. "What can I do? Where do you want me? How can I make this as successful as possible?"

Those are the ones I hire over and over again. Those are the ones I recommend to my planner friends. Those are the ones who become part of my circle. I have speakers who are now consulting with my clients as experts in their different areas, and they may meet with them 3-4 times a year. And my clients are now their clients too, with my blessing. I'm delighted to see them succeed, because they've proven themselves. They've done a stellar job but have also shown themselves to be a part of the team.

Shawna: So, you hit upon something great. If they behave like they're there to be helpful to you, not the other way around, that's huge. The less they need from you onsite, the more you are going to like them. Because they are self-sufficient, they are not expecting anything. They come in, they're professional enough to have communicated their needs in advance, provide their own dongles, talk to the A/V person, solve as many problems as they can, before getting you to stop what you're doing to serve them.

Tracey: I like how you used the word 'stellar.' As in Stellar Meetings and Events.

Bonni: Yes. As the name of my company, I try to use it ad nauseum. This is stellar coffee. Those shoes are stellar! But I digress.

I try to get as much information from speakers before we arrive onsite, so I can serve them in a way that helps them, and helps the meeting become more successful. So, I want to know what their A/V needs are. One of my favorite things about you as a speaker, Shawna, is that there's a page on your website that says, "For Meeting Planners," and it's got your bio and your A/V needs and all of that stuff on there, which is epic.

Every speaker should do that. If not, it's really as simple as an email or a conversation where I say, "Hey, what do you need? This is what we've got onstage. Is there more that you need?" And don't say you want different kinds of lighting, different staging, don't get silly. If I say I have two Lavalier mics and a handheld and a podium mic, just tell me which one of those you want. Don't tell me you want a boom and a spotlight and a laser show unless you're joking. Then please tell me that. Because funny always works for me.

I'm going to ask you what you like to drink, I'm going to make sure you have everything you need. Really, above all, at this point you are my guest just like everyone else in the room. I want you comfortable, but low maintenance.

Tracey: How do you feel about warm nuts?

Bonni: In my personal life, or in terms of this conversation?

Tracey: Yes. And wafting.

Bonni: Big fan of the wafting. Never have warm nuts at my meetings. Our speaker/planner friend Tracy Stuckrath would tell you nuts are a mistake at meetings. And she'd be right.

Shawna: Yes, you have to be wary of the people with nut allergies.

Bonni: Yes. That's a pet peeve of meeting planners. My first thought when Maralynn said that was "No, no, not nuts!"

Shawna: My inner 12-year-old boy just keeps snickering at the combination of words.

Bonni: My inner 12-year-old boy has been with you from the beginning.

Maralynn: So, what we've established is that if you need wafting, then I'm your gal. Also, that it all comes back to the fact our industry is relationship-based, no matter how hard certain corporate behemoths are trying to change it. That's always the way it's going to be.

I'm going to hire someone who I trust, that I've built a rapport with, and as a speaker, it behooves you to figure out a way to bond with your planner, and not be an obstacle. The more that you position yourself as an accessible expert, the more we'll dig you. That's when I'm going to tell everyone I know about you. That's when I'm going to recommend you. That's when you're going to be top of mind, because you stood out in my mind for the right reasons.

If we've created some sort of a bond, and you are an expert in your field, then I'm going to preach that to whoever I can. People on the street. They're just going to be walking by and I'm going to tell them about you. But, it's something that I think people forget. They get so tied up in their own head with, "I need to elevate myself, I need to be better than everyone else." But you still need to be able to relate to the peons. So, figure it out.

Shawna: So what you're saying Maralynn is, you better check yourself before you wreck yourself?

Maralynn: Bingo. There you go being "street" again.

Shawna: I can't help it.

Bonni: Yes. I hire people that I like, and who respect what I do, because I can't have people walk in and call me Diet Coke all the time. I am also a professional. I am not the receptionist for the meeting.

Shawna: No, you ain't, girl!

Maralynn: I'm the designer of the meeting. I'm the creator of the meeting, and I'm the partner to my clients. I'm also their gatekeeper. And I can be yours as well, during the program, but a little mutual respect goes a long way. All planners know, whether we choose to wield the power or not, that we can make or break your success. We can make things extremely difficult for you, or we can make them a freakin' cakewalk. It's up to you how you want to do this dance. You give me respect, I'll give you respect.

If you bring 30 people with you, we're going to have an issue, and even if I have extra seats, they may mysteriously not be available. There's a degree of respect that we need to show each other, and oftentimes planners are treated as implementers, even by speakers. We're treated as the person who can get coffee, or Diet Coke, or wafting popcorn. But we are experts in our field, and it will make your life a whole lot easier if you can figure out a way to create a relationship with us.

Shawna: The most ironic thing of all is the people who really need to read this chapter...will never read this chapter.

Tracey: Truth.

Maralynn: I think maybe we should have some of these top-line items made into stickers. We can have them in the back of this book, so planners can just peel off a sticker and just smack it on the person's forehead and say, "This is for you."

Shawna: Maybe we can just print this particular chapter, and deliver it under their ice-cold Diet Coke, and their warm nuts.

Bonni: I see that as an epic room delivery.

Maralynn: I would pay at least $5 for that room delivery. At least.

Shawna: Yeah, I'll pay your $10,000 fee once, Jerk Speaker, but the $5 I pay to deliver your warm nuts and your chapter on diva behavior is far more...

Bonni: Priceless.

Shawna: Keynote speaker: $10,000, Room drop: $5, Getting in the last word: Priceless.

Maralynn: Priceless. That's exactly what I was just going to say.

Bonni: And while we're on the topic of diva behavior and not treating the planner with disrespect, please remember we know everybody in the hotel, from the bellperson to the front desk person, to the person who is parking your car, to the person who is cleaning your room. They are part of the team that is making the program work. We, as planners, make it a point to be as respectful as possible to everyone in the hotel, and if you're disrespectful at the front desk and throwing diva behavior around there, believe me, they're going to tell me, and believe me, it will be reflected in your Diet Coke, your wafting nuts, and your...what else did we ask for?

Maralynn: And your recommendations.

Bonni: And your recommendations. I will surely tell other planners if you're rude to hotel staff. I send my own staff home for that.

Shawna: Let's share some more horror stories.

Tracey: I booked a speaker one time who was a celebrity. A comedian, Gilbert Gottfried. And really, at the time, I cautioned my client about booking this guy, because in the case of comedians in particular, there are people who tend to be a little crazy on stage, very unpredictable on your stage. And Gilbert Gottfried got on stage at an awards dinner, so it was a big dress up affair. And he proceeded to use expletives and he used...I mean he made religious jokes, he was just in general, rude. And after about 20 minutes, the host of the event, got up and took him out. He said, "We're done here." And so then I got a call the next day from the client, and they wanted a refund. And I'm like, "I think I warned you about this guy."

And so we didn't end up refunding money after that, but it could have been, we could have had to give it back. And so it was bad all the way around. There have been other speakers who were just...it was all about them when they were there, you know. And they were wonderful on stage and did their presentation perfectly. But then, they get off stage, and now it's all centered on them, and how we can service them, and how come no one's talking to them, and how come this, that and the other. And it's just like, "Are you kidding me? You know, this is not about you, you are just a one-time little piece of this event."

Shawna: It's even funnier when they're a breakout speaker, like the diva with her entourage.

Tracey: But one who was absolutely wonderful was Henry Winkler. His agent told us time and time again, in no uncertain terms, that we were not to try to schmooze him, we were not to try to get people to meet-and-greet him. We couldn't ride in a car with him. I mean, he was just like in this little bubble, and we were just supposed to move the bubble over to the stage and put him on stage.

In reality, he could not have been nicer. I mean, he is the most down-to-earth man I have ever met in my entire life, particularly for a celebrity. And not only did I ride in the car with him at his invitation, he is the one who signed 400 books after the show.

He also asked us to take him to a barbecue place there in Fort Worth. And so we did. He shook hands with everybody in the restaurant. The cook came out, the guy who made the fricking barbecue, the brisket, came out all sweaty and dripping with meat grease, and said, "Mr. Winkler, I want to shake your hand." And it was overwhelming. And Henry got up and talked to the guy one-on-one. He sat there with us for a couple hours at lunch before we had to take him to the airport. I mean, he just was the absolute nicest man I've ever, ever worked with, and I will recommend him till the day I die, or till the day he dies, whichever comes first.

Shawna: So if Henry Winkler doesn't act like a...

Maralynn: A Divo?

Shawna: Seriously? A male diva is called a divo? Mind blown.

Maralynn: That's the correct term. It's Italian.

Shawna: So, if Henry Winkler doesn't act like a divo, then some self-important nobody who wants his nuts warmed, or his Diet Coke, has no business being a divo.

Bonni: And I think there's a lesson here about your speakers bureaus and your agents. Make sure that they are representing you for who you are. Because we can come up with some negative preconceived notions based on the way you've been presented. And sometimes they're just looking to protect you, but yeah, I mean, that's a perfect example of an agency gone awry and misrepresenting. I had a similar experience with a speaker who I absolutely adored, but who I was not looking forward to meeting because of barriers that had already been put up. He turned out to be epic, and I've already hired him again.

Shawna: There was a speaker, just a regular guy. Seemed like a nice enough guy. When he arrived on site, he and his wife checked into their room. And it was the wife who called one of our staff people who was in charge of sleeping rooms. And she was pissed, because they expected a room with a view, and she, "had to crook her neck to be able to see the ocean." Not kidding. And she made the speaker look like a complete jerk, when it was the spouse.

Maralynn: Yeah, pick your spouses wisely, speakers. That's the advice that we have for you. So I had someone who was presenting, who did an excellent job, but was a complete a-hole when not presenting. And at one point, he was up on stage and he was rehearsing. And there was an A/V crew member who was sitting to the side, sort of going over notes. And the speaker actually said, "That person. Could you please have that person go somewhere else, because they're in my sight line and it's very distracting."

This was someone who was working and was going over notes about the speaker and what we were going to do. You know, almost like script supervising basically, and just trying to go over things. And the first thing I thought to myself is, "Who are you, the friggin' Pope? Like, what makes you more special than anybody else?" I mean, one of the things we find as planners, and also just as human beings, is the most compelling person is someone who's relatable and someone we can connect with. You could be the greatest speaker on stage, but if you can't figure out how to be a human with some compassion, you're not going to get very far with us. We're all going to tell each other about you.

Bonni: We can hear each other's voices going up when we tell these stories, you can't hear it in the book. But, even retelling the stories, the emotion is coming out.

Tracey: So true. So very, very true.

Shawna: Bonni, you need to tell the story about Rob Lowe.

Bonni: Ah, Rob Lowe. I think Tracey and Shawna were both with me for this one. We were in the audience of a large conference filled with thousands of meeting planners from every walk of society. Rob Lowe was one of the speakers. The meeting was set up in an interview format.

I'm going to get way politically incorrect, but I'm doing it as part of the story. The interviewer asked him what it was like to work with children when he was in one of his sitcoms. And he responded that, because of the child labor laws, "We had to bring in midgets, and they would get under the covers, and we'd all be in bed snuggling up, and they would get really inappropriate." And he went on and on: crazy midgets this, and horny midgets that. And the interviewer kept saying, "Little people." And he kept going, "Yeah, midgets." And it just kept going back and forth, he kept saying, "Midgets," in this very disparaging way, and the interviewer kept going back to, "Little people."

At some point, after being corrected for the billionth time, Lowe said, "Relax, it's not like they're in the room." And the emcee said, "Well actually, we do have a group of planners from the Little People of America here." Everybody stood up and cheered. And this group of little people, who ran programs for Little People of America got up and took a bow. That was a really bad moment for Rob Lowe. And he laughed and said, "What are the odds?! They're going to kill me on social media tomorrow," instead of, "I'm sorry." Good lord, people, know your audience. And be respectful with your language.

Shawna: I will never forget, number one, "What are the odds?!" And number two, the fact that he never apologized. So you know, if you make a grievous mistake on stage, just own it. I once made a horribly inappropriate joke on stage at a religious conference. I can't be trusted in certain circles. But I quickly apologized and moved on. Funny I was never hired back. Hmmm.

Bonni: Funny. And you know what? Be politically correct. Show some respect for everyone when you're on stage. Even if you're kind of a jerk in real life, don't bring that to the stage. Everyone knows the proper term for little people is little people. So if you're going to be on a stage with 3,000, or even three people in front of you, use the socially acceptable terminology and show a little respect.

Shawna: Yes, it all comes down to respect, which has really been a thread throughout this book. Meeting planners want to be treated with respect, and we'll treat you with respect until you're a jerk. It's really just all about that at the end of the day. And that's how we develop relationships. That's how we get to know and like you enough to refer you and trust that you'll make us look good if we do refer you.

Tracey: I also want to add, in the same light, the respect. Also understand that most planners, I would say 99% of us, are going to do whatever we can to make that meeting a success. It may not be pretty behind the screen, or behind the curtain, but it will be pretty when our people see it. Don't add to the craziness we have to deal with.

Bonni: I have three short not-to-do stories: We were having a meeting, and one of the topics touched on environmental issues. There was a large group of audience members who were in the energy industry, and one of our speakers went through a long, drawn out story about the Exxon Valdez and shredded the oil industry. This was years after the disaster. Someone got up in the audience, and said, "Well, I'm in the energy industry and..." And he shut him down. And then a few other people got up and made some comments in defense of the energy industry, and he started an argument with them. People walked out. It was mortifying. And in the end, everyone hated him. He could have been great. He was awful. Don't fight with the audience. Again, know your audience.

Shawna: Wow.

Bonni: The second lesson: respect your audiovisual team. I am never, ever going to forget the speaker who yelled, "Next slide, next slide, next slide, Jesus Christ, next slide!" after a 10-second delay in transition. This sort of thing will always show you as unprofessional. Whatever she was intending to get across when she 'Next Slided' was lost in the tantrum. She came across looking like a mad woman, and really depressed the audiovisual team and the planners. Because we all want you to look great. Even if we hate you, we want you to look great. Because it's our meeting, and we need you to look great.

Shawna: The next time I see you in person, I'm going to scream, "NEXT SLIDE!"

Bonni: I will hug you anyway.

And then my big horror story, my biggest speaker horror story ever was with Jonah Lehrer. Jonah had written a book called, *How We Decide*. We were doing a meeting titled, "Mistakes, Decisions and Learning." We had this whole brilliant concept all laid out, and it was right when his new book, *Imagine*, had come out.

The meeting was about a month out, I was in Scotland at another meeting, and I opened up my iPad to read this news aggregator I read at that time. The headline on page one was *Lie, Lehrer, Lie*. It was an article about how he had recycled his blog for half of the book and invented the other half. He made up entire conversations with Bob Dylan about writing "Like a Rolling Stone," and Dylan called him out on it. When he got caught, he defended himself and lied. It went on for months. By the time I saw the article, his publisher had fired him, taken back his advance and pulled his book from the shelves. It took him months to finally admit it. Of course, the subtopic of this conference was working ethically.

Art Caplan who was the ethicist to Bill Clinton, and the go-to ethics guy in the world, was our emcee for the meeting. Luckily, the speakers bureau helped to find another speaker who was spectacular, who was able to step in and did a fantastic job. But that headline...that was one of the most stressful moments of my career. So the takeaway was don't lie, don't plagiarize!

TOP TAKEAWAYS

1. Respect your audience. Use appropriate language and know that anyone can be in the room at any time.
2. Don't lie and/or plagiarize.
3. Trite is trite is trite. Try not to repeat oft-used phrases. Because what goes around, comes around. And there's no I in team.
4. NEXT SLIDE!!!!

BONUS TIP: If you don't want us to call you Diet Coke, Warm Nuts, Wafting Popcorn or Fancy Pants behind your back...Shawna "Street" Suckow says you betta check yourself before you wreck yourself.

Chapter 16:

And So We Close…

"So long, Partner."
- Tom Hanks as Woody in "Toy Story 3"

Shawna: Ladies, any closing thoughts now that we've come to the end?

Tracey: I have loved working on this book with you three! It's gritty and real, and sometimes really gritty. But, the truth is, we want to work with fabulous speakers who want to help our meetings be bad-ass and successful. If you can do that for me, the world is your oyster. Dammit, now I'm hungry again.

Maralynn: Talk/writing this book with you three ladies has been a blast and a half and I'm so proud of us broads! Being candid is my favorite and I think we delivered that here. Being even more candid is actually my real favorite, but that can't be printed...think of the children! Now, where's my cake??

Bonni: With all due respect to other projects, this one has been the most fun of all. Big thanks to Tracey, Shawna & Maralynn, who found the time to make this happen. I'll not speak of iguanas again.

Shawna: I want to thank each of you for doing this, for sharing your wisdom so candidly and openly. I know it's going to help a lot of my speaker friends to be more successful. You rock! Let's go have cake.

ABOUT THE AUTHORS

MARALYNN ADAMS, CMP

Maralynn was a poor sharecropper's daughter...wait, that's not right. Maralynn grew up in the Northern California Bay Area and after a butt load of junior golf and working in golf shops, she decided to jump over to the dark...I mean corporate...side. After an eye-opening stint as an Executive Assistant, she learned that the wondrous, cotton candy world of event management existed after being thrown into the deep end to plan a 300-person conference for a huge-mongous company (with no prior training). She still attends therapy to deal with the trauma of that first meeting. A mere 13 years of planning on the corporate side helped propel her into becoming an independent corporate event director of her very own company, which just celebrated its ten-year anniversary. She loves taking care of her clients almost as much as she loves cake.

Stop with the staring. We get it...you need more info about the ridiculously adorable doggo above. Meet Martini the Wonderdog, the Chief Barketing Officer of The Corporate Event Group LLC. Martini just celebrated her 19th birthday and she and her sassy underpants are still going strong!

In her spare time (you can stop laughing now), Maralynn produces and occasionally acts in independent films. In the last five years, she's helped create 16 films and although her sweet mother doesn't understand why Maralynn loves being so sleep-deprived, she shows no signs of stopping. Her proudest accomplishment in the film arena is writing and producing her very own movie in 2018. Shockingly, it's an inappropriately hilarious comedy. Go figure.

BONNI SCEPKOWSKI, SFP

Bonni started her career with the intention of teaching children with special needs. This education comes in surprisingly handy almost daily in her work. After running travel departments for various corporations, she eventually fell face first into meeting planning, when her clients began asking her to plan meetings for them as well.

Using 'fake it 'til you make it' as her mantra, she figured it out as she went along with a lot of help from friends. This might explain her unorthodox style and the lack of letters after her name. Eventually she found her niche in strategic meeting management, which merges her love of the creative with her passion for bossing people around. Bonni founded Stellar Meetings & Events in 2000, almost accidentally, and has truly found her calling.

A serendipitous crossing of paths with Shawna Suckow at a train station changed everything. Bonni joined SPIN and, as Tracey so eloquently put it, found her tribe. They are her friends, her family and her board of directors. When not planning meetings, Bonni enjoys travel, pina coladas and getting caught in the rain. Wait- that's my match.com bio. When not planning meetings, Bonni enjoys travel, hanging out with her SFP Heath and her pugs. A perfect day would be spent with her daughter and grandkids who are smarter and better looking than most.

TRACEY SMITH, CMP, CMM

Tracey didn't start out to be a meeting planner. She thought she wanted to be in public relations, which is kind of close. After bouncing around from one job to another, she landed at a software company in Dallas writing technical documents. You know, user manuals that no one ever reads.

But the stars aligned, and Smith began working in the Marketing Department coordinating the company's trade shows.

Someone asked if she could plan a user conference, and she said sure. She eventually planned user conferences for more than 1000 clients. Smith had found her purpose and her tribe. She hired speakers for all of these conferences, using a speakers bureau in Dallas. After being laid off from the software company, Smith joined the bureau as a sales rep in 2006. Her first client was Shawna Suckow, a friend she met through MPI when she moved to Minnesota.

Suckow founded SPIN in 2008 and Smith joined the association as its very first member. Smith and Suckow together planned the first three annual conferences, winning an award for most innovative event in 2011.

Smith decided to go back to meeting planning and joined American Express Global Business Travel Meeting and Events as a corporate meeting manager for three years. Smith enjoyed her clients, but she needed something more.

Suckow approached Smith about taking on the Executive Director position in the summer of 2017, but Smith wasn't initially ready. After a few months, though, she decided this was the piece missing from her career and began as the Executive Director of SPIN January 1st, 2018. Smith says it's the cherry on the sundae that has been her three-decade career.

Smith would write more books, but her dog Carly needs to go out. Again.

SHAWNA SUCKOW, CMP, SFP

Shawna is a recovering 20-year meeting planner. Like the other ladies, planning fell into her lap, and she loved it. She spent seven years as a corporate planner before relocating to Minnesota and founding her own company in 1999. In 2008, she inadvertently created SPIN, which today has become an association of 2,500 senior-level meeting planners across North America. Back then, she would rather have swallowed glass than speak on a stage. But as the founder of an association, people wanted her to frequently stand up and say words. Out loud.

Eventually, Shawna fell in love with speaking (especially once she realized she could get paid for it). Since 2012, she's been a professional speaker focusing on consumer behavior, helping organizations in 16 countries (and counting!) understand how to connect & sell better to them in today's rapidly evolving marketplace.

Shawna hopes to impress you by sharing that she's a best-selling author who's written three previous books on buyers and sellers and the chasm between them. Three cool things you might not know about Shawna: She played in the World Series of Poker Main Event (the one on ESPN), she's an exceptional parallel parker, and she once did a terrible turkey impersonation for Jimmy Kimmel's audience. #fail